QUOTABLE ROYALTY

Quotable ROYALTY

by
Carole McKenzie

MAINSTREAM
PUBLISHING

EDINBURGH AND LONDON

Also available by the same author:

Quotable Women
Quotable Sex
Quotable Scots

Copyright © Carole McKenzie, 1993
Illustrations © Carolyn Ridsdale, 1993
All rights reserved

The moral right of the author has been asserted

First published in Great Britain in 1993 by
MAINSTREAM PUBLISHING COMPANY
(EDINBURGH) LTD
7 Albany Street
Edinburgh EH1 3UG

ISBN 1 85158 575 3

A catalogue record for this book is available from the
British Library

Typeset in Sabon by Litho Link Ltd, Welshpool,
Powys, Wales
Printed in Great Britain by Mackays of Chatham plc,
Chatham

ACKNOWLEDGMENTS

The wisdom of the wise and the experience of the ages are perpetuated by quotations.

Benjamin Disraeli

A special thanks to Alison Payne and Carolyn Ridsdale who helped with the words and pictures. Also to the library staff of London and Thames Valley libraries.

PREFACE

There is not a single crowned head in Europe whose talents or merit would entitle him to be elected a vestryman by the people of any parish in America.
Thomas Jefferson *(1743-1826)*

This is a unique collection of quotations. It is a compilation of remarks, witticisms, judgements and platitudes by and about royalty from throughout history. Many have been selected for their historical interest – that is, for the light they throw on some important figure or event or on some attitude current at the time. Others have been chosen purely for fun.

In making even a cursory examination of the quotations in this book, one cannot fail to be impressed by the number of parallels of events. History does, it seems, repeat itself:

A royal mistress should curtsy first then jump into bed.
Alice Keppel, *mistress of King Edward VII*

. . . My great-grandmother was your great-great grandfather's mistress. How about it?
Camilla Parker-Bowles, *to Prince Charles on their first meeting in the 1960s. (Her great-grandmother was Alice Keppel)*

The 1990s have seen great changes in the style of British monarchy. This more accessible image has placed the Royal family under a microscope as never before: their every action is covered in detail by the media, and family and marital dramas are revealed for all the world to observe and comment upon. Queen Elizabeth II herself acknowledged 1992 as an *annus horribilis*, a particularly eventful year for the Royal family.

Let them cant about decorum
Who have characters to lose.
Robert Burns *(1759-96)*

Someone once said that there is nothing certain but change. As we approach the twenty-first century there will be many more changes in the monarchy. Meanwhile I hope that you find this book an entertaining read, and keep in mind the words of Thomas Carlyle:

History, a distillation of rumour

ABDICATION

The Allied powers have proclaimed that the Emperor Napoleon is the sole obstacle to the re-establishment of peace in Europe, he, faithful to his oath, declares that he is ready to descend from the throne, to quit France, and even to relinquish life, for the good of his country.
Napoleon I *(1769–1821), Act of Abdication, 4 April 1814*

I now quit altogether public affairs, and I lay down my burden.
Edward VIII *(1894-1972) in his abdication speech, 1936*

I have found it impossible to carry the heavy burden of responsibility and to discharge my duties as King as I would wish to do without the help and support of the woman [Wallis Simpson] I love.
Edward VIII *in a radio broadcast, December 1936*

His Majesty has given the matter his further consideration but regrets he is unable to alter his decision.
Edward VIII's *reply to the Cabinet who had asked him to reconsider his intention to abdicate*

Bertie arrived very late from Fort Belvedere and Mr Walter Monckton brought him and me the paper drawn up for David's abdication of the throne of this Empire because he wants to marry Mrs Simpson!!!!!
Queen Mary *(1867–1953), Queen Consort to George V, diary entry, 9 December 1936*

Well, Mr Baldwin! this is a pretty kettle of fish!
Queen Mary, *referring to the abdication of Edward VIII*

Our cock won't fight.
Lord Beaverbrook *(1879-1964), Canadian-born newspaper proprietor, to Churchill during the abdication crisis*

7

ACTING

I'm glad you like my Catherine. I like her too. She ruled thirty million people and had three thousand lovers. I do the best I can in two hours.
Mae West (1892-1980), *speaking from the stage after her performance in Catherine the Great*

The King and Duke of York was at a play; but so great performance of a comical part was never, I believe, in the world before as Nell hath doth this, both as mad girle, and then, most and best of all, when she comes in like a young gallant; and hath the motions and carriage of a spark, the most that ever I saw any man have.
    It makes me, I confess, admire her.
Samuel Pepys (1633-1703), *diarist, on seeing Nell Gwyn play Florimel in Dryden's* Mayden Queens, Diary, *2 March 1667*

He had so natural an aversion to formality . . . he could not on premeditation act the part of a king for a moment, either in Parliament or Council . . . which carried him into the other extreme . . . of letting all distinction and ceremony fall to the ground, as useless and foppish.
John Sheffield, Earl of Mulgrave (1648-1721), of Charles II

ACTION

However brilliant an action it should not be esteemed great unless the result of a great motive.
François, Duc de La Rochefoucauld (1613-80), writer

We would often be ashamed of our finest actions if the world understood all the motives which produced them.
François, Duc de La Rochefoucauld

My words are my own, and my actions are my ministers'.
Charles II (1661-1700), *replying to Lord Rochester*

George I was lazy and inactive even in his pleasures, which therefore were lowly sensual. He was coolly intrepid and intently benevolent . . . Importunity alone could make him act, and then only to get rid of it.
Lord Chesterfield *(1694-1793), English statesman, of George I*

AD LIB

My husband is going to give my speech.
The Queen, *on discovering that she had forgotten her reading glasses just before she was due to give a speech in the Guildhall, June 1993*

ADULTERY

No proof of her guilt her conduct affords,
She sleeps not with courtiers, she sleeps with the Lords.
Lord Holland, *(1773-1840), epigram, after Queen Caroline had been asleep during the first day of her trial for adultery, August 1819*

ADVICE

First health, then wealth, then pleasure, and do not owe anything to anybody.
Catherine the Great *(1729-96)*

Don't worry about things you cannot alter.
Catherine the Great

Do not tell secrets to those whose faith and silence you have not already tested.
Elizabeth I *(1533-1603)*

Beware of enjoying mean acts.
Empress Maria Teresa *(1717-80), to her son, King Joseph II*

Never make a defense or apology before you be accused.
Charles I (1600–49), *letter to Lord Wentworth, September 1636*

Better have as king a vulture advised by swans than a swan advised by vultures.
Panchatantra (c. fifth century), tr. Arthur W. Ryder

Had I been present at the creation, I would have given some useful hints for the better ordering of the universe.
Alfonso X (Alfonso the Wise) king of Leon and Castile (1221-84), attrib.

An army marches on its stomach.
Napoleon I, attrib.

Keep your bowels open sir.
The ship's (HMS Bronington) *medical assistant to Prince Charles when he left the navy, December 1976*

I have nothing to tell you, but remember this, my last words – never again make a woman regent and ruler of China. It is against the house-law of our dynasty and should be forbidden. Be careful not to let the eunuchs meddle in government matters. The Ming dynasty was brought to ruin by eunuchs, and its fate shall be a warning to my people.
Dowager Empress T'Zu Hsi of China (1835-1908)

After that breathtakingly bad taste visit to the Florida Everglades Club, which refuses entry to those of the Red Sea pedestrian persuasion . . . and . . . gives the Hebraic warnings against contact with things porcine, it might be wise for all remotely Jewish people to avoid the Duchess altogether.
Julie Burchill, The Mail on Sunday, 1992

Whatever happens to him in his present capacity as royal poor relation can't do him much good in the long run. My advice to him would be: give up being a royal personage, stick to the sea, learn a trade and find an anchorage with an average wife.
Daily Worker, 1946 of Prince Philip, Duke of Edinburgh

I'm prepared to take advice on leisure from Prince
Philip. He's a world expert on leisure. He's been
practising for most of his adult life.
Neil Kinnock, *1981*

AFFAIRS

I don't remember any love affairs. One must keep
love affairs quiet.
The Duchess of Windsor *(1896-1986)*

James was naturally candid and sincere and a firm
friend, till his affairs and his religion wore out all his
first principles and inclinations.
Gilbert Burnet, *(1643-1715), Bishop of Salisbury, of
James II*

The whole affair has lasted since 16 November, and
is very painful. It is a terrible blow to us all, and
particularly to poor Bertie.
Queen Mary, *December 1936, referring to the affair
between Edward and Mrs Simpson*

AGEING

Get up dear, you're older than I am.
The Queen Mother, *to Evelyn Laye (in her eighties) when
she curtsied*

Brother I am too old to go again to my travels.
Charles II, *replying to Lord Rochester*

Queen Victoria in her eighties was more known,
more revered, and a more important part of the life
of the country than she had ever been. Retirement
for a monarch, is not a good idea.
Prince Charles

Command has aged me
Prince Charles, *leaving the navy, December 1976. In true naval tradition, a lavatory seat was placed round his neck, adorned with dangling toilet rolls. He was then pushed in a wheelchair (bearing the above banner), to his car*

I have only been in the navy five years, and sometimes I feel 80 already. I'm sure I have aged about ten years since I took command. I don't know why my beard hasn't turned grey.
Prince Charles, *to Mayor Reginald Dunkley, after sailing HMS* Bronington *into the docks at Barry, Glamorgan, 1976*

The years that a woman subtracts from her age are not lost. They are added to the ages of other women.
Diane de Poitiers *(1499-1566), mistress of Henri II of France*

A I D S

It could be said that the AIDS pandemic is a classic own-goal scored by the human race against itself.
Princess Anne

She doesn't just go and shake hands with someone who's got AIDS to prove it's OK to shake hands; she actively goes to other countries to see how things are, and she marches around on foot to see for herself.
Audrey Slaughter, *Ex-Editor of* Vanity Fair, *of Princess Anne*

A L L E G A T I O N S

That was the worst thing that has happened in my life. It came totally out of the blue. As children we had been brought up with stories of 'The Trial' told by my mother and old servants.
Princess Michael of Kent, *of media accusations that her father had been a member of the SS*

AMBITION

He is every way a perfect Stuart, and hath the
advantage of his brother only that he hath ambition
and thoughts of something he hath not, which gives
him industry and address even beyond his natural
parts. Yet his conduct, courage, judgement and
honour are not much to be confided in. His religion
suits well with his temper; heady, violent, and
bloody, who easily believes the rashest and worst of
counsels to be most sincere and hearty . . . His
interest and design are to introduce a military and
arbitrary government in his brother's time.
Anon., *of James II and VII, report drawn up for the Earl of
Shaftesbury, 1850*

I agree I am ambitious, and I don't see that as a
pejorative term. I want to do the best I can whatever
it is I'm doing. I didn't realise my life would be like
this when I married. I expected to be what we are,
junior members of the Royal family. I suppose it
was having been married before, although my first
marriage was annulled, and, most of all, being a
Catholic, that attracted attention.
Princess Michael of Kent, *speaking of media interest in
her* Good Housekeeping *interview, September 1992*

I should like to be a horse.
Queen Elizabeth II, *when asked about her ambitions as a
child, attrib.*

ANGER

I sometimes feel like shooting the Queen's corgis.
Princess Michael of Kent

Anger makes dull men witty, but it keeps them poor.
Elizabeth I

I may be pale, but it is from anger at being obliged
to see the King of Prussia, and not from cold.
Queen Alexandra *(1844-1925), Queen Consort to
Edward VII*

ANXIETY

Great events make me quiet and calm; it is only
trifles that irritate my nerves.
Queen Victoria *(1819-1901), letter to King Leopold of*
Belgium, April 1848

APPEARANCE

Oh Philip, do look! I'm wearing my Miss Piggy face.
The Queen, *on seeing herself on television*

When I appear in public people expect me to neigh,
grind my teeth, paw the ground and swish my tail –
none of which is easy.
Princess Anne

Such an active lass. So outdoorsy. She loves nature
in spite of what it did to her.
Bette Midler, *of Princess Anne*

She is not one of the handsomest women in the
world. She has a swarthy complexion, long neck,
wide mouth, bosom not much raised, and in fact has
nothing but the King's great appetite, and her eyes,
which are black and beautiful and take great effect.
Report of the **Venetian Ambassador**, *on Anne Boleyn, to*
Henry VIII

If Cleopatra's nose had been shorter the whole face
of the world would have changed.
Blaise Pascal *(1632-62), French philosopher and*
mathematician

I remember the first time I saw Prince Philip. He was
playing on a rope hanging from a tree, and he had
this incredibly white, white hair.
Jim Orr, *recalling when he met Philip (then a pupil at*
Gordonstoun). Later he became a private secretary to the
Prince

I shouldn't have got it cut – my husband will kill me.
Duchess of York, *speaking to a crowd, about her hair,*
March 1991

I thought it was time I had a spring clean and had it cut short. Never mind, it will always grow back again.
Duchess of York, *revealing that her new look hadn't met with her husband, Prince Andrew's approval, April 1991*

The mere idea would make him ill. The Prince wears a white silk crêpe evening shirt and a narrow unlined barathea silk tie. The shirt is very fine and you couldn't wear a tie with a thick band or adjustment underneath it. He wears a single-ended bow tie, as it is neater.
Kenneth Williams, *Managing Director of the Prince's shirt makers, Turnbull & Asser, referring to Prince Charles and denying the suggestion that Charles wears a clip-on or pre-tied bow*

. . . Her face oblong, fair but wrinkled; her eyes small, yet black and pleasant; her nose a little hooked, her lips narrow and her teeth black (a defect that the English seem subject to from their too great use of sugar) . . . She wore false hair and that red.
Paul Hentzner, *German tutor to Queen Elizabeth I*

After you have met 150 Lord Mayors, they all begin to look the same.
George V *(1865-1936), attrib.*

She was in low stature, and what the French call mignonne and piquante, well formed, handsome but red-haired; and rather embonpoint; of the endue she was a complete mistress. Airing, fantastic, and sprightly, she sang, danced, and was exactly made for acting light, showy characters, filling them up, as far as they went, most effectually. On the front of Bagnigge Wells, one of her country houses, where she entertained the King with concerts, there was a bust of her, and though it was wretchedly executed, it confirmed the correctness of Lely's pencil. She had remarkably lively eyes, but so small they were almost invisble when she laughed; and a foot, the least of any woman in England.
Anon., The Manager's Note-Book, *describing Nell Gwyn*

He's ugly and crooked
His nose it is hooked
The devil to him is a beauty
Nor father nor mother
Nor sister nor brother
Can ever bring him to his duty
Anon., *referring to William III, c.1688*

He has gotten in part the shape of a man,
But more of a monkey, deny it who can;
He has the tread of a goose, and the lags of a swan,
A dainty fine King indeed.
Anon., *coronation ballad, referring to William III, 1689*

He had a thin and weak body, was brown haired,
and of a clear and delicate constitution.

He had a Roman eagle nose, bright and sparkly
eyes, a large front, and a countenance composed to
gravity and authority.

All his senses were critical and exquisite. He was
always asthmatical, and the dregs of the small pox
falling on his lungs, he had a constant deep cough.

His behaviour was solemn and serious, and
commonly with a disgusting dryness, which was his
character at all times, except in a day of battle, for
then he was all fire, tho' without passion; He was
then everywhere, and looked to everything.
Gilbert Burnet, *referring to William III*

I was asked in Australia whether I concentrated on
improving my image – as if I was some kind of
washing powder, presumably with special blue
whitener. I dare say that I could improve it by
growing my hair to a more fashionable length, being
seen at the Playboy Club at frequent intervals and
squeezing myself into excrutiatingly tight clothes
. . . but I intend to go on being myself to the best of
my ability.
Prince Charles *to an interviewer, before his marriage*

There was a seam in the middle of his fore-head,
(downwards) which is a very ill sign of
Metoposcopie.
John Aubrey *(1626-97), English antiquary and folklorist,
of Charles I*, Miscellanies

Never have I beheld features more unfortunate.
Gianlorenzo Bernini *(1598-1680), sculptor, attrib. on seeing Van Dyck's* Charles I, in three positions

Those who knew his face, fixed their eyes there; and thought it of more importance to see than to hear what he said. His face was as little a blab as most men's, yet though it could not be called a prattling face, it would sometimes tell tales to a good observer. When he thought fit to be angry, he had a very peevish memory; there was hardly a Blot that escaped him.
George Savile, *Marquis of Halifax (1633-95),* A Character of King Charles II

. . . looked lonely and wistful as all the males of this family do on State occasions.
Henry Channon, *(1879-1958), British writer, observing the King's (George VI) first levee (assembly of visitors),* Diary, *6 February 1937*

The King James, with his large hysterical heart, with his large goggle-eyes, glaring timorously-inquisitive on all persona and objects, as if he would either look through them, or else be fascinated by them, and, so to speak, start forth into them, and spend his very soul and eyesight in the frustrate attempt to look through them, – remains to me always a noticeable, not unloveable, man. For every why he has his wherefore ready; prompt as touchwood blazes up, with prismatic radiance, that astonishing lynx-faculty.
Thomas Carlyle *of James I of England and VI of Scotland, (1795-1881), writer,* Historical Sketches

Tall and severe as a cathedral.
A pupil's description of *Anne de Beaujeu, Duchess de Bourbon, daughter of Louis XI and sister of Charles VIII*

Marguerite's masculine attire suits her well, and her Adonis face is so bewildering you cannot tell if she is

male or female. She could easily be a charming boy as the beautiful lady she is.
Pierre de Bourdeille, Seigneur de Brantome (c.1540-1614), *contemporary chronicler of Marguerite, sister of Louis XII*

Pretty, witty Nellie at the King's house.
Samuel Pepys, *describing Nell Gwyn aged 15*

His nose and mouth are too enormous and he pastes his hair down on his head and wears his clothes frightfully – he really is anything but good looking.
Queen Victoria, *describing her son, Edward VII*

A gentleman does not indulge in careless self-indulgent ways, such as lolling in armchairs or on sofas, slouching in his gait, or placing himself in unbecoming attitudes with his hands in his pockets. He will borrow nothing from the fashion of the groom or the game keeper, and whilst avoiding the frivolity and foolish vanity of dandyism, will take care that his clothes are of the best quality.
Prince Albert (1819-61), *consort to Queen Victoria, introduction in a briefing document to equerries entitled* Appearance, Deportment and Dress

Man in crowd to Princess Diana: You really are gorgeous
Diana's riposte: Don't let my better-half hear that
Incident when Charles and Diana opened an exhibition at Broadlands, 1981

From his childhood this boy will be surrounded by sycophants and flatterers by the score, and will be taught to believe himself as of a superior creation.
Keir Hardie (1856-1915), *Labour politician, on the birth of the future King, Edward VIII*

ARCHITECTURE

Why can't we have those curves and arches that express feeling in design? What is wrong with them? Why has everything got to be vertical, straight, unbending, only at right angles and functional?
Prince Charles

A large number of us have developed a feeling that architects tend to design houses for the approval of fellow architects and critics – not for the tenants.
Prince Charles

. . . A jostling scrum of office buildings so mediocre that the only way you ever remember them is by the frustration they induce – like a basketball team standing shoulder to shoulder between you and the *Mona Lisa*.
Prince Charles, *referring to the buildings surrounding St Paul's Cathedral, December 1987*

You have to give this much to the Luftwaffe – when it knocked down our buildings it did not replace them with anything more offensive than rubble. We did that.
Prince Charles, *the* Observer, *'Sayings of the Week', December 1987*

Like a carbuncle on the face of an old and valued friend
Prince Charles, *referring to a proposed modern extension to the National Gallery, 1986*

ARISTOCRACY

The brood of that dutiful and pleasant gentlewoman Elizabeth II and her immediate connections is now distending the country with a new and brazen aristocracy; a *nouveau ancien* regime.
New Statesman, *1986*

An aristocracy in a republic is like a chicken whose head has been cut off: it may run about in a lively way, but in fact it is dead.
Nancy Mitford, *British writer,* Noblesse Oblige

19

ART

The works of art, by being publicly exhibited and offered for sale, are becoming articles of trade, following as such the unreasoning laws of markets and fashion; and public and even private patronage is swayed by their tyrannical influence.
Prince Albert, *referring to the Great Exhibition, a display of the industrial products of Britain and Europe that he had organised, May 1851*

Paint her with oyster lip and breath of fame.
Wide mouth that 'sparagus may well proclaim
With Chanc'llors belly and so large a rump,
There (not behind the coach) has pages jump.
Andrew Marvell *(1621-78), English poet, of Anne Hyde, Duchess of York,* Last Instructions to a Painter

I am having a go at sketching, but Queen Victoria definitely was a very fine, talented artist.
The Duchess of York, *1992*

I am accustomed in any way to unveiling busts . . . I now complete the process of helping my father to expose himself.
Prince Charles, *unveiling a Vasco Lazzolo sculpture of his father at the Royal Thames Yacht Club*

AUDACITY

Excuse me Ma'am, will you sign my copy of the Morton book?
Passenger on flight BA4733, Edinburgh to London shuttle, to Princess Diana, 1992

Princes, learn not art truly but the art of horsemanship. The reason is, the brave beast is no flatterer. He will throw a Prince as soon as his groom.
Ben Jonson, *(1573-1637), English dramatist*

Fear created Gods; audacity created kings.
Prosper Jolyot de Crébillon *(1674-1762), French dramatist,* Xerxès *(1714)*

AUSTRALIA

If I were Australian, I would be thinking very hard
about the problem and what they are going to do.
The Duchess of Kent *on tour of Queensland, responding
to questions on the debate on whether Australia should
become a republic*

All the faces here this evening seem to be bloody
poms.
Prince Charles *at an Australia Day dinner, 1973*

AUTHORITY

It is no bad thing to be a king – to see one's house
enriched and one's authority enhanced.
Homer, *Greek poet,* Odyssey, c. *ninth century* BC

AUTOCRACY

I shall maintain the principle of autocracy just as
firmly and unflinchingly as it was upheld by my own
ever-to-be remembered dead father.
Nicholas II, *Tsar of Russia, (1868-1918), declaration to
representatives of Tver, 17 January 1896*

AVOIDANCE

The Queen: Sugar, Sugar, where are you Sugar.
Prince Philip: That, is Lilibet's (Queen Elizabeth II)
dog-defence mechanism going into play. If she
doesn't want to commit herself she calls the dog.

BACHELORHOOD

I have not yet met the girl I want to marry.
Prince Charles, *17 June 1977, the day the* Daily Express
*'officially' announced his engagement to Princess Marie-
Astrid of Luxembourg*

21

I have read so many reports recently telling everyone who I am about to marry that when last year a certain young lady was staying at Sandringham a crowd of about 10,000 appeared when we went to church. Such was the obvious conviction that what they had read was true that I almost felt I had better espouse myself at once so as not to disappoint too many people.

Prince Charles, *addressing a luncheon of the Parliamentary Press Gallery, referring to Lady Jane Wellesley*

Napolean returning from the Russian Campaign

BEAUTY

Of course an attractive girl of 26 will have had
previous boyfriends.
The Queen Mother *on press interest in Sarah Ferguson's
former boyfriends at the time her relationship with Prince
Andrew was made public*

To live and to die beautifully is the science of
sciences.
Christina of Sweden (1626-1689)

At last, as if in mockery of them, she came sailing up
the river Cydnus, in a barge with gilded stern and
outspread sails of purple, while oars of silver beat
time to the music of flutes and fifes and harps. She
herself lay all alone under a canopy of cloth and
gold, dressed as Venus in a picture, and beautiful
young boys like painted cupids, stood on each side
to fan her. Her maids were dressed like sea nymphs
and graces, some steering at the rudder, some
working at the ropes. The perfumes diffused
themselves from the vessel to the shore, which was
covered with multitudes, part following the galley
up the river on either bank, part running out of the
city to see the sight.
Plutarch (c. AD 46-119), *Greek biographer and author, of*
Cleopatra, Life of Mark Antony XXV

Yes I do think that the bloom of her ugliness is going
off.
Colonel Disbrowe, *chamberlain of Charlotte Sophia,
Queen Consort to George III (1744-1818), in William
Timbs's* A Century of Anecdote

Indeed I can never enough admire her beauty.
Samuel Pepys, *of Barbara Villiers, mistress of Charles II,*
Diary, 7 September 1661

Resident of old people's home to Princess Diana:
How beautiful you are. What is your secret?
Diana: Well, I must admit, partly make-up and I do
drink lots of water.

BED

The Duke of York hath not got Mrs Middleton, as I was told the other day, but says that he wants not her, for he hath others and hath always had, and that he hath known them brought through the Matted Gallery at White-Hall into his closet. Nay, he hath come out of his wife's bed, and gone to others laid in bed for him.
Samuel Pepys, *of James II*, Diary *24 June 1667*

Now, ladies and gentlemen, I wish you good-night. I will not detain you any longer from your amusements and shall go to my own, which is to go to bed; so come along, my Queen.
William IV *(1765-1837), to his guests at a party at St James's Palace*

BEHAVIOUR

She would not have become as bad . . . if my father [George IV] had not been infinitely worse.
Charlotte, Princess of Wales *(1796-1817), in Geoffrey Wakeford's* Three Consort Queens

Oh! deep was the sorrow and sad was the day,
When death took our gracious old Monarch away,
And gave us a Queen, lost to honour and fame,
Whose manners are folly, whose conduct is shame;
Who with aliens and vagabonds long having strolled loose,
Soon caught up their morals, brazen and bold.
Theodore Hook *(1788-1841), English playwright, on Queen Caroline in an imitation of Bunbury's 'Little Grey Man'*

Young Harry Killigrew is banished the Court lately
for saying that my Lady Castlemayne was a little
lecherous girl when she was young, and used to rub
her thing with her fingers or against the end of
forms, and that she must be rubbed with something
else. This she complained to the King of and he sent
to the Duke of York, whose servant he is, to turn
him away. The Duke of York hath done it, but takes
it ill of my Lady that he was not complained to first.
She attended him to excuse it, but ill blood was
made by it.
Samuel Pepys, *of Barbara Villiers, mistress of Charles II,*
Diary, *21 October 1666*

BELIEFS

To believe all is weakness; to believe nothing is
stupidity.
Christina of Sweden

BIRTH

May destiny, alloting what befalls,
Grant to the newly-born this saving grace,
A guard more sure than ships and fortress-walls,
The loyal love and service of a race.
John Masefield *(1878-1967), Poet Laureate, on the birth
of Prince Charles, 14 November 1948*

Freedom in Britain has grown and been safeguarded
under the ancient institution of the monarchy.
Declaration in the New York Herald Tribune *on the birth of
Prince Charles*

And art thou borne, brave Babe?
Ben Jonson, '*An Epigram on the Prince's [Charles II]
Birth*'

BLAME

We think Fergie did it.
Tony Banks, *Labour MP, jokingly implying the Duchess of York was responsible for the Windsor Castle fire, House of Commons, November 1992*

I don't blame you for the Windsor fire.
The Queen, *in a letter to the chief art restorer at Windsor Castle, absolving her of any blame, November 1992*

It was one of King Jame's maxims, to take no favourite but what was recommended to him by his Queen, that if she afterwards complained of this Dear One, he might answer. It is long of yourself: for you were the party that commended him unto me. Our old master took delight strangely in things of this nature.
Archbishop George Abbot, *of James I*

BOOKS

A strange, horrible business, but I suppose good enough for Shakespeare's day.
Queen Victoria, *giving her opinion of* King Lear

Oh, I've got that one! Unfortunately my husband disapproves. He doesn't like me reading light novels.
Princess Diana, *on visiting a hospital and seeing a Danielle Steele novel on a patient's bedside table*

Don't make me sound like a bookworm, because I'm not, but I'll read almost anything I can get my hands on, from women's magazines to Charles Dickens. I read because I enjoy it.
Lady Diana Spencer, *before her marriage to Prince Charles*

I found it difficult to believe that Morton would be given such information and made my own inquiries. At a reception in early March last year, I actually asked the Princess of Wales about the book. I told her that if it was not true it would be a most damaging and dangerous book.

In that conversation I was left in no doubt that she not only knew about the book, and what its contents were, but also did not feel it would be a danger to her.

Sir David Calcutt, *referring to Andrew Morton's book* Diana: Her True Story, Daily Mail, *January 1993*

Friedman is intrigued that the Queen carries her handbag to breakfast – exceedingly revealing given that a handbag is 'a universal symbol of security'.
Anthony Clare, *in a review of* Inheritance – A Psychological History of the Royal Family *by Dennis Friedman*, Sunday Times, *May 1993*

BRITAIN

Born and educated in this country I glory in the name of Britain.
King George III *(1738-1820)*

BUGGING

Ridiculous!
Prince Charles's *response to the allegation of bugging by MI5*

The prince is certain he has never been bugged by the security services.
Palace official

I am authorised to say that the stories of MI5 being involved in bugging members of the royal family are absurd.
Sir Antony Duff, *former Director General of MI5*

The Royal tapes are fakes.
To be blunt, they are a dog's breakfast.
Mr A. Morton, *forensic linguistics expert, Glasgow University*, Observer, *May 1993*

Diana: For once stop being so self-centred. You still think of me as the person you married.
Charles: I stopped thinking like that years ago.
Diana: Yes, I suppose that would be a good indication of why we drifted apart, my dear.
Charles: Tell me what it is you want me to say?
Diana: Say something I want to hear.
Charles: I'm leaving.
Diana: Oh, don't be so childish.
Charles: Oh God . . .
Excerpt from the Sun's *version of bugged conversation*

When you do a massive story like this it's very hard nailing down every single individual bit.
James Whitaker, *royal journalist when questioned by the media about the apparent inaccuracies in the bugging allegation story*

We are not only talking about somebody's job, we are possibly talking about their life involved in this. I am not prepared to put anyone's life on the line.
James Whitaker, *when asked to reveal his sources*

James hasn't got a clue how to handle a propelling pencil, let alone how to uncover the secrets of GCHQ.
Charlie Rae, *royal reporter,* Today

BUSINESS

. . . He spoke our language, but not well. His accent was foreign: his indication was inelegant; and his vocabulary seems to have been no larger than was necessary for the transaction of business.
T.B. Macaulay *(1800-59), British historian, of William IV*

CAMILLAGATE

Caller, said to be Prince Charles: Your great achievement is to love me. I adore you. I'm so proud of you.
Reply by woman, said to be Camilla Parker-Bowles: Love you forever
Extracts from a taped conversation said to be between **Prince Charles** *and* **Camilla Parker-Bowles**. *(Both deny they are lovers, but confess to being very good friends)*

I can't believe it. I can't believe it. I must speak to my husband. He is on his way home.
Camilla Parker-Bowles, *on hearing the news that details of the alleged conversation between herself and Prince Charles had been reported in an Australian magazine*

In light of the claims and counter-claims over the royal couple's relationship being made in the world media, we felt the public should be made fully aware of the complete content of the tape. We see this as a legitimate journalistic exercise.

Bob Cameron, *Managing Editor (News) New Idea magazine, statement, explaining why the magazine gave full details of the alleged relationship between Prince Charles and Camilla, 13 January 1993*

Office photocopiers whirred into overdrive throughout the capital as fax lines to Australia were commandeered for 'research' purposes.

Evening Standard, *reporting that London's business world were faxing colleagues in Australia for information on the Camillagate tapes*

CANADA

It makes little difference; Canada is useful only to provide me with furs.

Madame de Pompadour *(1721-64), mistress of Louis XV, on the fall of Quebec*

CARE

My care is like a shadow in the sun – Follows me flying – flies when I pursue it.

Elizabeth I, *on the departure of Alençon, 1582*

CHANGE

I'm less spontaneous but only because I'm more aware of my responsibilities. Andrew and I don't really have any hobbies together.

I find weekending the worst. When he goes away for a long period of time you know you're not going to see him for six or eight weeks, and then we'll see him at the end – fine. But weekends are difficult because he's working Monday through Friday, he comes back tired on Friday night.

The Duchess of York, *talking in an interview with* Hello *magazine about the strain on her marriage and how she has changed as a person, August 1990*

In many ways the royals have the instinct of a chameleon. They change their colours to live another day.

Harold Brooks Baker, *royal historian, speaking of how the Royal family must change in order to survive*

She [the Queen] has now paved the way for the Royal family to survive into the twenty-first century.

Harold Brooks Baker, *royal historian, referring to the Queen's decision to pay tax*

The assembly hall at school was dominated by the Annigoni portrait of Elizabeth II. God Save the Queen, we sang, and meant it. We learnt nothing of the naughtier side of monarchs such as George IV, his riotous life, his gluttony and gambling, wining and wenching.

Mike Carlton, *presenter on LBC Newstalk Radio, commenting in the* Sunday Times *on how the monarchy has changed since he attended school*

Most of the British diseases are spread by the existence of the monarchy, which personifies the notion that the divisions in society are divinely ordained and proclaims the virtues of tradition, when what the country needs is unity and change. But nobody really believes that Parliament will pass a United Kingdom [Abolition of the Monarchy] Bill in the foreseeable future. Nor is the Queen likely to abdicate and persuade her whole line of heirs and successors to do the same.
Roy Hattersley, MP, Daily Mail, *1992*

If the monarchy is to survive, it must consciously abandon the more blatant manifestations of an ancient class division. The Opening of Parliament need not be accompanied by middle-aged ladies-in-waiting dressed in mid-morning as if they were going to a charity ball, an ancient admiral holding aloft a sword which is almost too heavy to carry, or the Lord Chancellor perilously backing down the steps that lead from the throne.
Roy Hattersley, MP, Daily Mail, *December 1992*

This book comprises an intriguing collection of 'royal' cartoons mostly from the past 25 years, and shows the changes which have taken place in that period in both style and approach to the subject.
Prince Charles, *foreword to a collection of cartoons of royalty, 1978*

CHARACTER

Nothing could be more amiable and agreeable than she was. Can anyone wish for a better account of a little tit of 18 made all at once into a Queen?
Thomas Creevey *(1766-1838), British politician and diarist, of Queen Victoria in a letter to Elizabeth Ord, August 1838*

A king is not allowed the luxury of a good character. Our country has produced millions of blameless greengrocers, but not one blameless monarch.
King Magnus in The Apple Cart *by* **George Bernard Shaw** *(1856-1950)*

The qualities of Caroline of Ansbach were not moral qualities . . . but they were of a piece with the physical fortitude that had always upheld her . . .
   Through force of circumstances, her proceedings were often devious, but in a certain robust integrity she never failed and, though she dissimulated she remained obstinately and grandly herself.
Peter Quennell, *British author, of Queen Caroline*

George the First knew nothing and desired to know nothing; did nothing and desired to do nothing; and the only good thing that is told of him is that he wished to restore the crown to its hereditary succession.
Samuel Johnson *(1709-84), British writer, in James Boswell's 'Life of Johnson'*

Content to bargain for the gratification of his two predominant passions, Hanover and money, he was almost indifferent to the rest of his royal authority, provided exterior observance was not wanting; for he comforted himself if he did not perceive the diminution of Majesty, though it was notorious to all the rest of the world.
Horace Walpole, *referring to George I,* Memoirs

The Oxford Dictionary does not define the word 'twerp'. Webster's Third New International Dictionary defines a 'twerp' or 'twirp' as an 'insignificant or contemptible fellow'. Chambers Twentieth-Century Dictionary says it could mean a 'cad'. And the Penguin English Dictionary says it means 'a silly fool; an unimportant person' . . .

I do not think any of the above descriptions fit. I therefore take this opportunity of publicly and unreservedly apologising for so describing the Prince [Charles] in the House of Commons. I believe him to be a sensible, contented, pleasant young man. Who wouldn't be with a guaranteed untaxed annual income of £105,000?

Introducing a Bill to take the Duchy of Cornwall and its assets into public ownership in 1975, **Willie Hamilton**, MP, *called the Prince of Wales, a 'young twerp'. He was subsequently obliged to withdraw the remark in Parliament and further apologised in a letter to the* Times

Nor warp'd by passion, aw'd by rumour,
Not grave thro' pride, or gay through folly.
An equal mixture of good humour,
And sensible soft melancholy.
Alexander Pope *(1688-1744), English poet 'To a Certain Lady at Court', referring to Henrietta Howard, Countess of Suffolk*

He praised and reprimanded, rewarded and punished, with the stern tranquillity of a Mohawk chief.
T.B. Macaulay, *referring to William III*

There was no doubt to which type King George belonged. Without any attempt to make himself cheap or popular in a common way, he appealed to the most vital of his subjects. In character and convictions he was the averge Briton of his day, or what the average Briton aspired to be. He was John Bull.
John Brooke, George III

He was certainly a Sybarite, but his faults were
exaggerated. He was to the full as true a man as his
father. He would embrace you, kiss you – seized on
the Duke of Wellington and kissed him. He certainly
could be the most polished of gentlemen, or the
exact opposite.
Lord Aberdeen *(1784-1860), of George IV*

An omniscient umpire whom no one consulted.
Hugh Trevor-Roper, *historian, of James I and VI*,
Archbishop Laud

I do affirm that he was the most honest and sincere
man I ever knew: a great and good Englishman, and
a high protector of trade, and had nothing so much
at heart as the glory and strength of the fleet and
navy.
Thomas Bruce, *Earl of Ailesbury, of James I and VI*,
Memoirs

That character, almost devoid of the humanity and
kindliness which we appreciate most of all in kings,
seemed like a grim edifice or institution, divided into
separate, independent compartments, connected by
a few corridors, and known to the world only from
its cold, forbidding antechamber.
David Ogg, *of William IV*

The King can be explosive and denunciatory, but
always with a twinkle in his eye.
John Buchan *(1875-1940), Scottish novelist and
statesman, of George V*

The personality conveyed by the utterances that are
put into her mouth is that of the priggish school girl,
captain of the hockey team, a prefect, and a recent
candidate for confirmation.
Lord Altrincham's *impression of Queen Elizabeth
published in the* National and English Review, *August 1957*

He was the pluckiest and most determined patient I
ever had.
Lionel Logue, *speaking of the Duke of York. In 1926 he
taught the Duke how to gain confidence in public speaking*

Opinions of Queen Elizabeth II:

She is a woman who acts her age, which is 50. She has, in fact, acted that age since she was little more than 20.
Fern Marja Eckman, New York Post, *1976*

A very pleasant middle to upper-class type of lady, with a talkative retired Navy husband.
Malcolm Muggeridge, Saturday Evening Post

She is frumpish and banal.
Malcolm Muggeridge, *1957*

A piece of cardboard that they drag round on a trolley.
Johnny Rotten, *1977*

The working girl's Adam Faith.
Bud Flanagan, *of Prince Philip*

Diana: 1. Roman goddess of hunting.
      2. British goddess of shopping and film premières.
Mike Barfield, *The Oldie, 1992*

Foggy – dense and wet.
Princess Diana, *of Captain Mark Phillips*

CHILDBIRTH

The Queen of Scots is lighter of a fair son, and I am but a barren stock.
Elizabeth I, *at the time of the birth of future James VI*

If men had to have babies they would only ever have one each.
Princess Diana, *July 1984*

Dr Snow gave that blessed chloroform and the effect was soothing, quieting and delightful beyond measure.
Queen Victoria, *describing her labour*, Journal, *1853*

A little boy was born, weighing nearly eight lb at 3.40 a.m. Everything most satisfactory, both doing well. Sent a number of telegrams, had something to eat. Went to bed at 6.45, very tired!
The Duke of York *(later to become King George V), on the birth of his son, the future King George VI on 14 December 1895,* Diary

Darling May was safely confined of a son at 3.30 this morning both doing well.
Georgie
The Duke of York, *in a telegram to Queen Victoria on the birth of his son, 14 December 1895*

CHILDREN

The thing that impresses me most about America is the way parents obey their children.
Duke of Windsor

I cannot consent to be separated from my son. I can feel no enjoyment without my children; with them I can regret nothing.
Marie Antoinette, *Queen of France (1755-93), on the day of Louis XVI's execution*

How sharper than a serpent's tooth it is
To have a thankless child.
Lear in King Lear *by* **William Shakespeare** *(1564-1616)*

Children are not chores, they are part of us. If we gave them the love they deserve, they would not try so hard to attract our attention. If this empty cavern waiting for affection remains unfilled, it will be filled in some other way.
Princess Diana, *addressing a London drugs prevention conference, November 1992*

Hugging has no harmful side-effects. If we all play our part in making our children feel valued the result will be tremendous. There are potential huggers in every household.
Princess Diana, *addressing a London drugs prevention conference, November 1992*

The children can't go without me. I can't leave the King and of course the King won't go.
Queen Elizabeth (*now the Queen Mother*), *referring to her husband, George VI, and their refusal to leave war-time London, 1941*

It is indeed a pity that you find no consolation in the company of your children. The root of the trouble lies in the mistaken notion that, the function of a mother is to be always correcting, scolding, ordering them about and organising their activities. It is not possible to be on happy friendly terms with people you have just been scolding.
Prince Albert, *in a letter to Queen Victoria, 1 October 1856*

I know most of you can't speak English but the pictures are quite funny.
The Duchess of York, *on a visit to Poland, meeting children and handing out copies of her* Budgie the Helicopter *book*

He's the first in our family to become a Marine.
Prince Philip, *referring to Prince Edward, speaking to American admiral, Sylvester Foley, whose own son was an officer in the US Marines*

You're so lucky, a daughter is just what I've been longing for.
Princess Diana *in a remark to her brother, Earl Spencer, and his wife on the birth of a baby daughter*

Yes, a daughter – William and Harry long for a younger sister.
Princess Diana *when asked if she would like another child*

William and Harry must now come first. They need lots of love. Children from broken families suffer badly. They get into all sorts of problems.
Dame Barbara Cartland, *British novelist, step-grandmother of Princess Diana, December 1992*

The Duke was immensely proud [of Princess Elizabeth]. He had a way of looking at her that was touching. But Margaret brought delight into his life. She was a plaything. She was warm and demonstrative, made to be cuddled and played with.
Marion Crawford, nanny to Princesses Margaret and Elizabeth (now Elizabeth II), referring to their relationship with their father, George VI

They love their Papa [Prince Andrew, Duke of York] because he's a lovely man and he deserves to be loved.
The Duchess of York, speaking of her children, Princess Beatrice and Eugenie, December, 1992

They are completely delicious. I want to eat them most of the time. I've tried to give them as much of a feeling of a normal childhood as possible.
The Duchess of York, speaking about her children in an interview on American television, December, 1992

What a beautiful baby. May I look more closely? You must be a very proud mother. Would you allow me to give you a portrait of my mother?
An incident described by Mrs Leah Kersh who met King Edward VII as she wheeled a pram along the sea-front at Hove. He gave her a gold sovereign, bearing the head of Queen Victoria

. . . My grandfather [George V] found it so easy to find fault with anyone, that what was probably a basic kindness was quite lost in his gruff exterior . . . I don't think he really cared much for children and he had a positive mania for punctuality.
The Earl of Harewood

The child to whom I was most drawn was Prince Albert – Bertie – although he was not a boy who made friends easily. Intensely sensitive over his stammer he was apt to take refuge either in silence – which caused him to be thought moody – or in naughtiness. He was more often in conflict with authority than the rest of his brothers.
Lady Airlie, lady-in-waiting to Queen Mary

CHIVALRY

I thought that ten thousand swords would have leaped from their scabbards to avenge even a look that threatened her with insult. But the age of chivalry is gone. That of sophisters, economics, and calculators has succeeded.
Edmund Burke *(1729-97), Irish philosopher and statesman, of Marie Antoinette*

CHOICE

When a woman remains single, the world assumes that there must be something wrong about her, that she has some discreditable reason for it.
Queen Elizabeth I

CHRISTMAS

Christmas brings its own painful stresses to so many people in need . . . the lonely, the confused and the simply unloved need help more than ever.
Princess Diana, *December 1992*

I hope you all have a good Christmas. But don't leave your shopping to the last minute like me.
Prince Charles, *joking with the crowd on a visit to Holyhead, December 1992*

COMMON MAN

Good ole Charley Windsor, a young feller who's really as common as a new shoe.
Description of Prince Charles on an American tour in the New York Sunday News, *1970*

An idol is not the worse for being coarse materials; a king should be a commonplace man. Otherwise he is superior in his own nature, and not dependent on our bounty or caprice.
William Hazlitt *(1788-1830), English essayist, 'On the Spirit of Monarchy', 1823*

COMMUNICATION

One of the reasons that we find so few persons
rational and agreeable in conversation is that there
is hardly a person who does not think more of what
he wants to say than of his answer to what is said.
François, Duc de La Rochefoucauld

Do you talk to your plants?
Princess Diana, *on a visit to India to the head gardener of
the Moghul garden*

As so often happens, I discover that it would have
been better to keep my trap shut.
Prince Philip, *after a disastrous tour of Australia and New
Zealand*

A man can be forgiven a lot if he can quote
Shakespeare in an economic crisis.
Prince Philip, *attrib.*

I would say somewhat, but I cannot utter it.
Henry, Prince of Wales (1594-1612), *on his deathbed.
The Prince died of typhoid fever, though many suspected
that he was poisoned by his father*

He speaks to me as if I were a public meeting.
Queen Victoria, *referring to Gladstone*

The Royal yacht *Britannia* had just been used as a
temporary refugee ship during the evacuation of
Aden. 'The story showed the Navy in a really good
light', said a reporter, who approached the Prince
hoping that he would make a positive comment. 'He
just turned and snapped "Fuck off". Then he
pressed his electronic buzzer and the police came
running.'
A British reporter *who wishes to remain anonymous, of
Prince Philip, Duke of Edinburgh*

Very lewd. Very German.
*An equerry of the Queen describing Prince Philip's dirty
stories told when dining with male friends at Balmoral*

COMPARISONS

How canst thou seriously declare
That George the Third
With Cressy's Edward can compare,
Or Harry? 'Tis too bad, upon my word:
George is a clever King, I need must own,
And cuts a jolly figure in the throne.
Peter Pindar, *pseudonym of John Wolcot (1738-1819),*
English satirist, of George III

. . . He is an immense improvement on the last
unforgiving animal [George IV]. This man at least
wishes to make everybody happy.
Emily Eden, *British-born Indian novelist, letter to a friend,*
August 1830

[Stanley Baldwin] thought the new King would have
a great deal to contend with. There's a lot of
prejudice against him. He's had no chance to
capture the public imagination as his brother did.
I'm afraid he won't find it easy going for the first
year or two.
Lady Airlie, *referring to George VI*

COMPLIMENTS

She isn't a bad bit of goods, the Queen; I wish all the
fleas in my bed were as good.
Miguel de Cervantes *(1547-1616), Spanish novelist*, Don
Quixote, *1605*

The Queen did fish for men's souls and had so sweet
a bait that no one could escape her network.
Sir Christopher Hatton *(1540-91), English courtier, of*
Elizabeth I

You are a very beautiful couple.
President Roh Tae Woo, *to Princess Diana when she*
visited Seoul with Prince Charles, November 1992

43

CONFESSIONS

I have done very wrong with the Prince of Wales.
Often and in open day.
Confession of Lady Mordaunt to her husband, Sir Charles,
who found letters from the Prince of Wales inside a locked
desk of his wife's

CONFUSION

Oh! my Lord . . . if this woman should die, what
scene of confusion will there be! Who can tell into
what hands the King will fall? Or who will have the
management of him? I defy the ablest person in this
Kingdom to foresee what will be the consequence of
this great event.
Sir Robert Walpole *(1676-1745), English statesman, of*
Caroline of Ansbach, Queen Consort to George II

CONTEMPT

It is my Royal and Imperial Command that you . . .
exterminate first the treacherous English, and . . .
walk over General French's contemptible little
army.
Wilhelm II, *King of Prussia and Emperor of Germany*
(1859-1941), referring to the British Expeditionary Force.
Veterans of this force became known as 'old contemptibles'.
The Times, *October 1914*

COSMOS

I rather feel that deep in the soul of mankind there is
a reflection as on the surface of a mirror, of a
mirror-calm lake, of the beauty and harmony of the
universe.
Prince Charles

COURAGE

Courage! I have shown it for years; think you I shall
lose it at the moment when my sufferings are to end?
Marie Antoinette, *on the way to the guillotine, 1793*

Let the boy win his spurs.
Edward III *(1312-77) replying to a suggestion that he
should send reinforcements to his son, the Black Prince,
during the battle of Crécy, 1346*

COURTESY

The civilities of the great are never thrown away.
Dr Johnson, *Memoirs of the King of Prussia, 1746*

Punctuality is the politeness of Kings.
Louis XVIII, *King of France, (1755-1824) now a favourite
saying*

Etiquette is a thing he cannot comprehend.
Charles Greville *(1794-1865), English memoir writer, of
William IV*, Diary, *24 July 1830*

COURTS

Courts are, unquestionably, the seats of politeness
and good breeding; were they not so, they would be
the seats of slaughter and desolation.
Lord Chesterfield, Letters, *1749*

The court does not satisfy a man, but it prevents him
from being satisfied with anything else.
Jean de la Bruyère *(1645-96), French writer, 'Of the
Court'*, Caractères, *1688*

If it was not for you we would forswear all Courts; and really it is the most mortifying thing in nature, that we can neither get into the Court to live with you, nor you get into the country to live with us; so we will take up with what we can get that belongs to you, and make ourselves as happy as we can in your house.
Alexander Pope, *letter to Mrs Howard (Countess of Suffolk), 20 June 1726*

COURTSHIP

He did not greatly court the ladies, nor had he a lavish affection unto many; he was manly and well fitted for venerial sports, yet rarely frequented illicit beds; I do not hear of above one or two natural children he had or left behind him. He had exquisite judgement by the eye, and physiognomy, to discover the virtuous from the wanton; he honoured the virtuous; and was very shy and choice in wandering those ways; and when he did it, it was with much cautiousness and secrecy, nor did he prostitute his affection, but unto those of exquisite persons or parts; and this the queen well knew, nor did she wink at it.
William Lilly *(1602-81), English astrologer, of Charles I*

CRISIS

What is the Royal scandal? Are we dealing with a single reliable fact? It's an incredible deluge of rubbish . . . a farrago of rubbish.
Max Hastings, *editor of the* Daily Telegraph, *referring to press disclosures about the state of the marriage of Prince Charles and Princess Diana*

The feeling within the Royal family is that the
Princess will never be forgiven for what they see –
despite her repeated denials – as 'shopping' them to
Mr Andrew Morton, a pushy tabloid vulgarian
from Leeds with a shaky grasp of social nuances.
Hugh Massingbred, *obituaries editor of the* Daily
Telegraph, *referring to Princess Diana, the* Spectator,
December 1992

It's like Kylie Minogue leaving *Neighbours*.
Australia is not deeply perturbed.
Mike Carlton, *presenter on LBC Newstalk Radio,*
commenting in the Sunday Times *on the Royal separation,*
December 1992

CROWN

Uneasy lies the head that wears a crown.
King Henry in Henry IV Part II *by* **William Shakespeare**

Within the hollow crown
That rounds the mortal temples of a king
Keeps Death his court.
Richard II in Richard II *by* **William Shakespeare**

Few men are fit to wear a crown.
Jean de La Fontaine *(1621-95)*

King Charles II was crowned at the very conjunction of the Sun and Mercury . . . As the King was at Dinner in Westminster Hall, it Thundered and Lightened extremely; the Canons and the Thunder played together.
John Aubrey, Brief Lives

When James II was crowned according to the Ancient Custom, the Peers go to the throne, and kiss the King. The Crown was almost kissed off his head. An Earl did set it right: and as he came from the Abbey to Westminster Hall, the crown tottered extremely.
John Aubrey, of James II and VII

I would sell London, if I could find a suitable purchaser.
Richard I (1157-99), *when raising money for the third crusade*

I have two huge lions tearing at my flanks, the so-called Emperor Otto and John, King of England. Both try with all their might to upset the Kingdom of France. I cannot leave the country myself or do without my son here.
Philip II, *King of France (1165-1223) explaining to Pope Innocent III his refusal to crusade against the Albigensian heretics*

DAMPER

I've been here over an hour and they haven't even put the record-player on yet. I'm sure I'm putting a damper on things. I think I'd better go so that they can start enjoying themselves.
Prince Charles, *to a fellow student at a party while studying at Cambridge*

DANGER

The danger to the country, to Europe, to her vast Empire, which is involved in having all these great interests entrusted to the shaking hand of an old, wild, and incomprehensible man of 82½, is very great!
Queen Victoria, *reacting to Gladstone's fourth and last appointment as Prime Minister in a letter to Lord Lansdowne, 12 August 1892*

DEATH

We should weep for men at their birth, not at their death.
Baron de Montesquieu *(1689-1755), French writer*

Use it for the good of my people.
Queen Anne *(1665-1714), on handing over the symbolic staff of the treasury to Lord Shrewsbury*

I am the first Queen of England to go to the scaffold – a doubtful distinction. I shall be a saint in heaven. I will be easily nicknamed 'Anne sans-tête'.
Anne Boleyn *(1507-36), wife of Henry VIII*

To the executioner: The executioner is, I believe, very expert, and my neck is very slender.
On the scaffold: O God have pity on my soul, O God have pity on my soul . . .
Anne Boleyn

I pray you despatch me quickly. Will you take the head off before I lay me down?
Lady Jane Grey *(1537-1554), Queen of England beheaded after nine days on the throne, to her executioner*

Monsieur I ask for your pardon. I did not do it on purpose.
Marie Antoinette, *after stepping on the executioner's foot on the platform of the guillotine*

All my possessions for a moment of time.
Elizabeth I

My God, have mercy on my soul, and on my poor people.
Last words of **William the Silent**, *Prince of Orange (1533-84), as he fell under his assassin's bullets*

A subject and a sovereign are clean different things.
Charles I, *on the scaffold, January 1649*

Nothing could part us while we lived, but death seems to threaten to divide us. You, a Roman born, have found a grave in Egypt. I, an Egyptian, am to seek that favour, and none but you, in your country.
Cleopatra, *Queen of Egypt (60-30BC)*

Augustus said he wished to see a King, not corpses!
Suetonius (c.69-c.122 AD), *Roman biographer and antiquarian, on being asked if he wished to see the tomb of the Ptolemies, as well as the sarcophagus of Alexander the Great*

This is the first pain she has given me.
Louis XIV *King of France (1638-1713), at the death of his cousin the, Infanta Maria Teresa, to whom he had been married for 23 years*

O Lord God, I have set my hope in thee!
My dear Jesus free me;
in these harsh fetters, in this miserable punishment,
I long for thee. Weary with sighs, on my knees I adore thee, sad implore thee to set me free.
Mary Queen of Scots (1542-89), *shortly before her execution*

Here lies poor Fred who was alive and is dead,
Had it been his father I had much rather,
Had it been his sister nobody would have missed her.
Had it been the whole generation,
so much the better for the nation,
But since it is Fred who was alive and is dead,
there is no more to be said.
Anon., *on the death of Frederick Prince of Wales, 1751*

I am dying with the help of too many physicians.
Alexander the Great (356-323 BC)

Chief of the Army.
Last words of **Napoleon I**

What tho' the royal carcase must,
Squeezed in a coffin, turn to dust?
Those elements her name compose,
Like atoms are exempt from blows!
Jonathan Swift *(1667-1745), English satirist, of Queen*
Caroline

She died eating and drinking;
died fast and fustie;
salacious; lecherous.
Anthony Wood *(1632-95), English antiquary, of Anne,*
Duchess of York, Life and Times, *March 1671*

His death saved the kingdom for his descendants.
Bishop William Stubbs *(1825-1901), English historian,*
of King John, The Constitutional History of England

He died in the beginning of his climacterial year,
fatal many times where killing directions in the
nativity threaten.
William Lilly, *of Charles I*

He nothing common did nor mean
Upon that memorable scene,
But with his keener eye
The axe's edge did try;

Nor call'd the Gods, with vulgar spite,
To vindicate his helpless right;
But bow'd his comely head
Down, as upon a bed.
Andrew Marvell, *of Charles I who was beheaded*

King Charles the First walked and talked
Half an hour after his head was cut off.
'Peter Puzzlewell', A Choice Collection of Riddles,
Charades and Rebuses

Ward of the Law! – dread Shadow of a King!
Whose realm had dwindled to one stately room;
Whose universe was gloom immersed in gloom,
Darkness as thick as life o'er life could fling,
Save haply for some feeble glimmering
Of faith and hope if thou by nature's doom,
Gently hast sunk into the quiet tomb.
Why should we bend in grief, to sorrow cling,
When thankfulness were best? Fresh-flowing tears,
Or tears, or where tears flow not, sigh succeeding
sigh, Yield to such after-thought the sole reply
Which justly it can claim. The Nation hears
In this deep knell, silent for threescore years
An unexampled voice of awful memory!
William Wordsworth (1770-1850), *English poet,* On the
Death of his Majesty (*George III*)

How shall we speak of an infinite loss . . . the un-
imaginable touch of fate that extinguishes an epoch,
that removes the central figure of all the world . . .
The golden reign is closed. The supreme woman of
the world, best of the highest, greatest of the good,
is gone. The Victorian age is over. Never, never was
loss like this, so inward and profound that only the
slow years can reveal its true reality. The Queen is
dead.
Anon., *of Queen Victoria,* Daily Telegraph, *23 January 1901*

Dear dead Victoria
    Rotted cosily
In excelsis gloria,
    And RIP.
And her shroud was buttoned neat,
    And her bones were clean and round,
And her soul was at her feet
    Like a bishop's marble hound.
Dorothy Parker (1893-1967), *American writer,* 'Victoria'

There exists no proof as
To who shot William Rufus
But shooting him would seem
To have been quite a sound scheme.
E.C. Bentley (1875-1956), *English journalist and novelist,*
of William II, More Biography

A few countrymen conveyed the body, placed on a cart, to the cathedral at Winchester, the blood dripping from it all the way. Next year the tower fell; though I forebear to mention the different opinions on this subject, lest I should seem to assent too readily to unsupported trifles, more especially as the building might have fallen, through imperfect structure, even though he had never been buried there.

William of Malmesbury (c.1093-1143), *English chronicler, of William II, Chronicle of the Kings of England, translated by J.A. Giles*

There is one certain means by which I can be sure never to see my country's ruin: I will die in the last ditch.

William III (1650-1702), *attrib., to the Duke of Buckingham*

Lauds be given to the father of heaven for now I know that I shall die here in this chamber, according to the prophecy of me declared that I should depart this life in Jerusalem.

Henry IV (1367-1413), *after being taken to the Jerusalem Chamber at Westminster Abbey*

At last, as he was praying before the shrine of St. Edward at Westminster Abbey, he was seized with a terrible fit, and was carried into the Abbot's chamber, where he presently died. It had been foretold that he would die at Jerusalem, which certainly is not, and never was, Westminster. But, as the Abbot's room had long been called the Jerusalem chamber, people said it was all the same thing, and were quite satisfied with the prediction.

Charles Dickens (1812-70), *English writer, of Henry IV,* A Child's History of England

For God's sake, let us sit down upon the ground, and tell
sad stories of the death of Kings:
How some have been depos'd; some slain in war;
Some haunted by the ghosts they have depos'd;
Some poison'd by their wives; some sleeping kill'd;
All murder'd.
King Richard II *in* Richard II, *by William Shakespeare*

The King is not likely to live more than 18 months. The end will probably come suddenly. The operation was six months too late.
Sir Harold Graham Hodgson, *Royal radiologist, referring to George VI, September 1951*

Weep not, friend for me, who dies innocent, by the lawless act of wicked men. My condition is much better than theirs.
Agis III *(d. c. 204BC), the first King in Sparta ever to be killed by the Spartans (addressing a sympathiser)*

If I feel in good form, I shall take the difficult way up; if I do not I shall take the easy one. I shall join you in an hour.
Albert I, King of Belgium *(1875-1934), before falling to his death (on the Rocher de Marches les Dames, a mountain in Belgium)*

More quickly . . . inside . . . carry me to the palace . . . there to die.
Alexander II, Tsar of Russia *(1818-1881). After several abortive attempts, the Nihilists finally succeeded in assassinating the Tsar by throwing a bomb under his carriage*

I always was beautiful.
Pauline Bonaparte *(1780-1825), Napoleon's favourite sister, a handsome, scandalous and vain woman*

The Empress rose as usual at six o'clock, drank her customary five cups of coffee, and then began the day's routine. She saw her lover and her secretary, gave him orders, and then asked to be left alone for a moment.

When the secretary re-entered her apartment, he found her unconscious before the door of the bathroom. She died the following evening.
A report on the last hours of **Catherine the Great**

Our warm devotion and all love and goodness in our power. Noble Prince, dear brother, it is proper that you should know that we fell ill last Monday, and though we have hope of weakness and sickness is going from bad to worse. Therefore we beg of you in all friendliness to send promptly one or two of your councillors here to Newmarket, so that if God the Almighty calls us, your brotherly affection may know what sort of departure we made.
Grand Duchess, Beatrix of Bavaria *to the Duke of Bavaria, Newmarket, 1447*

Don't be afraid.
Charles XII, *King of Sweden (1682-1718), trying to bolster the courage of his troops after he was struck by a bullet while inspecting the trenches during an attack on Norway*

So here it is.
Cleopatra, *said to have committed suicide by causing an asp to bite her breast. According to Plutarch, she uttered these words upon discovering the snake in a basket of figs*

Carry my bones with you on your march, for the rebels will not be able to ensure the sight of me alive or dead.
Edward I *(1239-1307), who died on an expedition to Scotland against Robert the Bruce, to his soldiers*

Into thy hands, oh Lord, I commend my spirit.
Charlemagne, *King of France, the first Christian emperor of the West*

My Lord, the crown which I have borne so long has given enough vanity in my time. I beseech you not to augment it in this hour when I am so near my death.
Queen Elizabeth I, *silencing the Archbishop of Canterbury who had been enumerating for her the great achievements of her reign*

Throw a quilt over it.
Frederick the Great, *King of Prussia (1712-85), half conscious and on his deathbed, on seeing one of his dogs shivering*

Wally! What is this? It is death. They have deceived me.
King George IV, *calling to his page*

It is nothing.
Henry IV, *King of France (1553-1610), after being stabbed in the heart by the religious fanatic, Ravaillac*

I die a Queen, but would rather die the wife of Culpepper. God have mercy on my soul. Good people, I beg you pray for me.
Catherine Howard *(1520-42), fifth wife of Henry VIII, convicted of adultery and beheaded. (Culpepper was her lover)*

Do not weep for me, nor waste my time in fruitless prayers for my recovery, but pray rather for the salvation of my soul.
Queen Isabelle of Spain *(1451-1504)*

O Lord; lay not this great sin to their charge.
King James II *of Scotland (1430-60), killed by the accidental bursting of a cannon during a siege of Roxburgh Castle*

Here lies Joseph, who was unsuccessful in all his undertakings.
Joseph II, *King of Germany (1741-90)*

I pardon him, but let him know that it is on his account that I am dying.
King Louis I, *King of France (778-840). Known as 'the Debonair', he had difficulty maintaining his authority. The activities of his rebellious son prompted these words*

I die innocent!
Messieurs, I am innocent of all that I am accused of.
I hope that my blood will cement the happiness of
the French people.
Louis XVI, *King of France (1754-93), on being found
guilty of treason and condemned to the guillotine*

I accept the wedding gift, nor it is displeasing if my
husband can give his wife nothing better. Say this,
however, that it would have been a more
honourable death if my wedding and my funeral
had been further apart.
Sophonisba *(d. c. 204 BC), the new bride of the Numidian
Prince Masinissa, was sent poison by her husband so that she
would not be taken alive by the Romans*

You give it to me to warm me, but it has kept me too
hot.
Stanislas I, *King of Poland (1677-1766). The former king
died as a result of burns received when his bathroom caught
fire*

I have nothing to tell you, but remember this, my
last words – never again make a woman regent and
ruler of China. It is against the house-law of our
dynasty and should be forbidden. Be careful not to
let the eunuchs meddle in government matters. The
Ming dynasty was brought to ruin by eunuchs, and
its fate shall be a warning to my people.
Dowager Empress T'Zu Hsi

Valet to Princess Diana: A ship is a prison with the
chance of being drowned.
Princess Diana: But will we sink with anyone we
know?
Conversation said to have taken place on the royal yacht
Britannia *during Princess Diana's honeymoon*, Daily Mail,
May 1993

DEBT

Monsieur de Montaigu, consider what I owe to God, the favour he has shown me and the great indulgence for which I am beholden to him.
Anne of Austria (1601-66), wife of Louis XIII, King of France, and court playgirl of George Villiers (Duke of Buckingham) and Mazarin (cardinal and minister), acknowledging her debt

DESCRIPTIONS

He has even been called dull. He was not dull; but he was cut off. His mind was isolated, and to a whole group of appreciations, impervious . . . complexity did not bewilder him, rather he missed it altogether . . . He could scheme with things, but not against schemers . . . He thought in straight lines.
Hilaire Belloc (1870-1953), Anglo-French writer and poet, of James II

The King Henry was wise, valiant, and generally fortunate. His wife, Queen Eleanor, brought a great portion (fair provinces of France), and a great stomach with her; so that it is questionable, whether her forward spirit more drove her husband away from her chaste, or Rosamond's fair face more drew him to her wanton embraces. His sons (having much of the mother in them) grew up, as in age, in obstinacy against him.
Thomas Fuller (1608-61), English antiquarian, of Henry II, Church History of Britain

He [Henry II] had an enormous paunch, rather by the fault of nature than from gross feeding. For his diet was temperate, and indeed in all things, considering he was a prince, he was moderate and even parsimonious. In order to reduce and cure, as far as possible, this natural tendency and defect, he waged a continual war, so to speak, with his own belly by taking immoderate exercise . . . At the first dawn of day he would mount a fleet horse, and indefatigably spend the day in riding through the woods, penetrating the depths of forests, and crossing the ridges of hills. On his return home in the evening he was seldom seen to sit down, either before he took his supper or after; for, notwithstanding his own great fatigue, he would weary all his court by being constantly on his legs.
Giraldus Cambrensis *(c. 1147-c.1223), Norman-Welsh historian,* The Conquest of Ireland, *translated from the Latin by T. Forester*

A bold merry slut who lay laughing there upon people.
Samuel Pepys'*s description of Nell Gwyn, mistress of Charles II,* Diary, *7 January 1669*

D E S T I N Y

He's not the sort of person to show his emotions. But you can tell from a man's face – how he sets his features. I'll never forget it. He looked as if half the world had fallen on him.
Michael Parker, *who roused Prince Philip from a nap to tell him that the King (George VI) was dead. The death of her father meant that Princess Elizabeth would become Queen and Prince Philip her consort*

He was born to be a salesman. He would be an admirable representative of Rolls-Royce. But an ex-King cannot start selling motor cars.
The Duchess of Windsor, *referring to her husband*

DETERMINATION

I must not take the easy way out.
Queen Elizabeth II *as a child*

Study mankind. Learn to use men without surrendering to them. Have confidence in those who, if necessary, are courageous enough to contradict you.
Catherine the Great

I am your anointed Queen. I will never be by violence constrained to do anything. I thank God I am endured with such qualities that if I were turned out of the realm in my petticoat I were able to live in any place.
Elizabeth I of England

I have often heretofore ventured my life in defence of this nation; and I shall go as far as any man in preserving it in all its just rights and liberties.
James II *(1633-1701), address to the Privy Council on becoming King, 1685*

In my view he who goes ahead is always the one who wins.
Catherine the Great, *letter to Baron F.M. Grimm, December 1793*

The bullet that will kill me is not yet cast.
Napoleon I, *at Montereau, 17 February 1814*

No, I shall not give in; I shall go on; I shall work to the end.
Edward VII, *the successor to Queen Victoria who earned the nickname Edward the Peacemaker*

I did very well, starting badly but finishing brilliantly.
Queen Victoria, *speaking of her attempts at dancing the waltz*

DISAPPOINTMENT

It's ruined my day.
Dr Julia Schofield, *expressing her disappointment at not being allowed to have her guide dog by her side when she received her MBE. One of her former guide dogs, Yates, had accompanied Dr Schofield to a Buckingham Palace garden party, and coped well: 'The Prince held out his hand to greet me, I held out mine, and the dog did the same. He put his paw in Charles's hand, and he shook it. And the same thing happened when we met Princess Anne.' November 1992.*

This is normal procedure. Investitures are important, formal occasions and it would simply not be appropriate to have guide dogs in the big room with so many people about.
A Palace spokesman, explaining the ban on guide dogs at investitures

DIVORCE

If you have a boil and it bursts, it often gets all right afterwards. Of course it won't end in divorce.
Lady Elmhirst, *the Duchess of York's grandmother, commenting on the adverse press publicity surrounding the Duke and Duchess of York's marriage, 1992*

Better than a play.
Charles II, *referring to a House of Lords debate on the Divorce Bill*

DRESS

In England, if you are a duchess, you don't need to be well dressed – it would be thought quite eccentric.
Nancy Mitford, *Noblesse Oblige, 1956*

She continued to hand on her clothes with her usual negligence when she was the King's mistress, but whatever she did became her.
James Granger *(1723-26), English biographer, of Nell Gwyn*, Biographical History of England

Then was there flowing hair and extravagant dress; and then was invented the fashion of shoes with curved points; then the model for young men was to rival women in delicacy of person, to mince their gait, to walk with loose gesture, and half-naked. Enervated and effeminate, they unwillingly remained what nature had made them; the assailers of others' chastity, prodigal of their own. Troops of pathics and droves of harlots followed the court.
William of Malmesbury, *describing the court of William II*, Chronicle of the Kings of England, *translated by J.A. Giles*

He [King George VI] was puzzled too, when a Cabinet Minister, Aneurin Bevan, declined to wear evening dress on the ground that it was an upper-class uniform.
Sunday Express, *September 1957, from A.J.P. Taylor*, The Improbable King

I am often asked, whether it is because of some generic trait that I stand with my hands behind my back, like my father. The answer is that we both have the same tailor. He makes our sleeves so tight that we can't get our hands in front.
Prince Charles, *at the annual dinner of the Master Tailors' Benevolent Association*

I ought to be wearing that. After all, I'm the Prince of W(h)ales.
Prince Charles, *on meeting Harry Secombe and noticing Secombe's tie which was decorated with whales*

DRINK

You can't drink a cup of tea to that.
Queen Victoria, *on hearing a drinking song by Rubinstein*

I thought I can't bear this any more and went off somewhere else. The only other place was the bar. Having never been into a bar before, the first thing I thought of doing was having a drink, of course. And being terrified, not knowing what to do, I said the first drink that came into my head, which happened to be cherry brandy, because I'd drunk it before when it was cold out shooting. Hardly had I taken a sip when the whole world exploded round my ears.
Prince Charles, *aged 14, referring to the occasion when he slipped into a hotel bar to avoid crowds of onlookers. The story appeared in newspaper reports all around the world*

DUTY

Everyone has to have a sense of duty. A duty to society, to their family. I mean, you name it. If you haven't got a sense of duty you get the sort of community we have now. Look around. Mugging and drugs and abuse – intellectual abuse, intellectual mugging!
Prince Philip, The Independent on Sunday

ECONOMICS

The biggest waste of water in the country by far.
You spend half a pint and flush two gallons.
Prince Philip

EDUCATION

The art of education is to combine formal training
with as wide a variety of experiences as possible,
including some which involve a calculated risk. I
think education is intended to produce intelligent,
morally strong, self-sufficient human beings willing
and capable of improving the machinery of living
which man has created for his enjoyment.
Prince Philip

Educate men without religion and you make them
but clever devils.
The Duke of Wellington (1769-1852)

Part of the royal education is
To be resigned
To your behind
Becoming numb
The worst of every coronation is
We always wish we hadn't come.
Noël Coward (1899-1973), *English actor, dramatist and
composer, 'Coronation Chorale', from* The Girl Who Came
to Supper

The King observing with judicious eyes,
The state of both his universities,
To Oxford sent a troop of horse, and why?
That learned body wanted loyalty;
To Cambridge books, as very well discerning
How much that loyal body wanted learning.
Joseph Trapp (1679-1747), *on George I's donation to
Cambridge University*

The King (George I) to Oxford sent a troop of horse
For Tories own no argument but force.
With equal skill to Cambridge books he sent,
For whigs admit no force but argument.
Sir William Browne (1591-1643), *pastoral poet, in a riposte to Trapp*

The natural honesty of his temper, joined with the narrow notions of a low education, made him look upon his acceptance of the crown as an act of usurpation, which was always uneasy to him.
Lady Mary Wortley Montague (1689-1762), *English writer, of George I*

The Duke of York was spoken of, as a well meaning and an honest man, but as one scarcely on a level with the ordinary scale of human intellect. Neither he nor his brother [George IV], however, had any proper knowledge of meum and tuum, a fault that was probably as much owing to the flatterers that surrounded them, as to defective education as to natural tendencies.
James Fenimore Cooper (1789-1851), *American writer, referring to the Duke of Albany and York, Frederick Augustus*

King George grunted and prodded the ground with his stick. At first acquaintance he was rather disconcerting. He had a loud, booming voice, rather terrifying to children and young ladies who did not know him. After a moment he said: For goodness sake, teach Margaret and Lilibet to write a decent hand, that's all I ask you. Not one of my children can write properly. They all do it the same way. I like a hand with some character in it.
Marion Crawford, *of George V*

I am afraid there is no disguising to you that P[rince] A[lbert] has gone a mucker. He has been quite off his head, with the excitement of getting home, for the last few days, and unfortunately as those were the days of the examinations, he has come quite to grief.
James Watt, *second master at Osborne to Mr Hansell, 1910*

Thank you. I am pleased with my boy.
King George V to the term officer, referring to Prince Albert's increased self-confidence

The difficulty in the education of a Prince, especially of the heir to the throne, is that he is forced too early into life, and that too much is expected of him.
Frederick Waymouth Gibbs, senior tutor to the future King Edward VII

The Queen and I want Charles to go to school with other boys of his generation and learn to live with other children, and to absorb from childhood the discipline imposed by education with others.
Prince Philip, on a visit to the USA, 1956

He is still a little shy, but very popular . . . passionately keen on and promising at games . . . academically, a good average . . . *Prince Charles's first end-of-term report from Cheam*

Question to Prince Philip: How's he getting on?
Prince Philip: Well, at least he hasn't run away yet.
The Prince was referring to the time spent by Prince Charles at Gordonstoun (1962-5)

Australia opened my eyes. Having a title, and being a member of the upper classes, as often as not militates against you there . . . Australia conquered my shyness.
Prince Charles, describing his time at Geelong school, Australia (1966-7)

I am one of those stupid bums who never went to university . . . and I don't think it's done me any harm.
Prince Philip

Poor little Wales,
Sure the saddest of tales
Is the tale of the studies
With which they are cramming thee.
Punch on the young Bertie, Prince of Wales

I have learned the way a monkey learns,
by watching its parents.
Prince Charles

EMBLEM

. . . . Rather a bad choice!
Princess Anne, *in reply to Prince Charles who had asked*
why the bald eagle had been chosen as the American national
symbol. Both were visiting a wildlife park near Washington
to witness the dissection of a bald eagle which had died from
organic pesticides, on a tour of the USA, 1970

Something about our national bird, and nobody's
quite sure what, was bugging our Royal visitors
from Great Britain.
The Washington Post *responding to Princess Anne's remark*
on the American national emblem

Every time I turn round 20 million reporters are on
my heels, and I can't get used to it.
Princess Anne, *explaining the pressure from the press led*
her to make the comment on the eagle

EMPIRE

How is my Empire?
King George V, The Times, *January 1936*

O' Sov'reign of an isle renown'd
    For undisputed sway
Wherever o'er yon gulph profound
    Her navies wing their way,
With juster claim she builds at length
    Her empire on the sea,
And well may boast the waves her strength,
    Which strength restor'd to Thee.
William Cowper (1731-1800), *English poet,* On the
Benefit Received by His Majesty George III from Sea
Bathing.

The German empire has become a world empire.
Wilhelm II, *Berlin, 18 January 1896*

ENEMY

Though I could not get them to stand against the enemy, I could not get rid of them now I had a mind to it.
Charles II, *in An account of His Majesty's Escape from Worcester Dictated to Mr Pepys 1680*

I don't know what effect these men will have upon the enemy, but by God, they terrify me.
The Duke of Wellington, *surveying his troops*

You have many enemies, that know not why they are so, like to village-curs, bark when their fellows do.
King Henry in Henry VIII *by* **William Shakespeare**

Good kings are the only dangerous enemies that modern democracy has.
Oscar Wilde *(1854-1900), Irish poet and dramatist, 1883*

France is invaded, I am leaving to take command of my troops, and, with God's help and their valour, I hope soon to drive the enemy beyond the frontier.
Napoleon I, *at Paris, 23 January 1814*

Personally, I feel happier now that we have no allies to be polite to and to pamper.
George VI, *to Queen Mary after the fall of France, 1940*

If I had my own way, each one of these would have Hitler's name on it.
Female worker in a munitions factory sorting out live bullets from dud ones, to George VI who was visiting

To have a good enemy, choose a friend: he knows where to strike.
Diane de Poitiers

ENGLISH

It is true that George III could only think of one thing at a time, but as that is also one of the most prominent characteristics of the English people, what might have proved a source of weakness served as an additional bond of union between him and them.
Sir Charles Petrie, The Four Georges

Had James ruled Spain, or even in seventeenth century France, history might now be resounding with his praises, voiced not only by Spaniards or Frenchmen, but by Englishmen. But as he ruled in England, he still waits his apologist.
David Ogg, *of James II,* England in the Reigns of James II and William III

No amount of human ingenuity can resurrect an extinct species, but it can defend one from extinction if enough forethought and determination are employed in its defence. I have always had an interest in wildlife – one which I have probably inherited from my father. I can never fail to be fascinated by and grateful for the incredible complexities of nature. A world deprived of any more of those animals would not be a world that I could care to extol.
Prince Charles, *foreword to* The Living World of Animals

EPIGRAM

Here lies, wrapt up in forty thousand towels,
The only proof that Caroline had bowels.
Alexander Pope, Epigram for Queen Caroline *(Caroline of Ansbach)*

EPITAPH

I do not want a lying official epitaph. Write on my tomb that I was a faithful servant of my master, the Emperor William, King of Prussia.
Prince Otto Von Bismarck *(1815-98), on his deathbed.*
Known as the Iron Chancellor and the peace-keeper of Europe, he served under William I and fell out with William II and resigned his post

ETIQUETTE

If you find you are to be presented to the Queen, do not rush up to her. She will eventually be brought around to you, like a dessert trolley at a good restaurant.
Advice in the Los Angeles Times, *1983*

My father told me that if I ever met a lady in a dress like yours, I must look her straight in the eyes. Otherwise someone might take a photograph of me in what might appear to be a compromising attitude.
Prince Charles *at a charity show at the Theatre Royal, Windsor to the actress, Susan Hampshire, (who was wearing a low cut, backless gown)*

You must never look at your feet, my mother always taught me that.
The Queen, *instructing a lady-in-waiting on how to come downstairs in a long dress with a train*

EULOGY

Next in the playhouse she took her degree
As men commence at University.
No doctors, till they've masters been before:
So she no player was till first a whore.
The Earl of Rochester *(1647-80), English courtier and poet, on the stage debut of Nell Gwyn,* Panegyrie on Nellie

Three white: the skin, the teeth and the hands.
Three black: the eyes, the eyelashes and the
eyebrows.
Three red: the lips, the cheeks and the nails.
Three long: the waist, the hair and the hands.
Three short: the teeth, the ears and the feet.
Three broad: the bosom, the forehead, the space
between the brows.
Three narrow: the mouth, the waist and the ankle.
Three soft: the fingers, the hair and the lips
Three small: the nipples, the nostrils and the head.
*A journalist's description of Lola Montez, mistress of King
Ludwig I of Bavaria. She was said to possess all these
attributes, except her eyes which were blue*

EVIL

T'is not enough (thy pietic is such)
    to cure the call's Kings Evill with thy touch;
But thou will yet a Kinglier, maistrietric,
    To cure the Poets Evill, Povertie,
And, in these cures, do'st so thy selfe enlarge,
    As thou dost cure our Evill, at thy charge . . .

What can the Poet wich his King may doe,
    But, that he cure the peoples evill too?
Ben Jonson, An Epigram to King Charles [I] for 100
pounds he sent me in my sicknesse

EXPECTATIONS

Well, since I see all the birds are flown, I do expect
from you that you shall send them unto me as soon
as they return hither.
*Charles I, on entering the House of Commons to arrest five
MPs, 1642*

The best, perhaps, that can be said of him is that on
the whole, all things considered, he might have been
worse.
*Justin McCarthy (1830-1912), Irish politician, novelist
and historian,* The Four Georges

FAIRNESS

My people and I have come to an agreement which
satisfies us both. They are to say what they please,
and I am to do what I please.
Frederick the Great of Prussia

I did not usurp the crown, but was duly elected.
Henry IV, *in reply to Richard Frisby, a Franciscan on trial
for plotting to overthrow him in 1402,* Eugologium
Historiarum

Everyone knows that I act in everything with
kindness and mercy, for I am forcing Rouen into
submission by starvation, not by fire, sword or
bloodshed.
Henry V *(1387-1422), to an envoy from Rouen, 1418*

FAMILY

We're not a family; we're a firm.
George VI *(1895-1952),* Our Future King *by Peter Lane*

If the immediate family breaks up, the problems
created can still be resolved, but only if the children
have been brought up from the very start with the
feeling that they are wanted, loved and valued.
Princess Diana, *addressing a London drugs prevention
conference, November 1992*

King William thinks all
Queen Mary talks all
Prince George drinks all
And Princess Anne eats all.
Anon., *shortly after the Glorious Revolution of 1688*

For too many a happy family remains a missed
opportunity. For many the sparkle has gone. Others
only become aware of what they really wanted to do
when it's too late.
Princess Diana, *February 1990*

Sadly, so often nowadays there is less and less
contact between generations. I have found it an
enormous benefit to be able to talk to my
grandmother and to my late uncle.
Prince Charles, *speaking at a ceremony to promote
solidarity between generations, December 1992*

One-parent families can work as well as those with
two . . . No longer should we be hoodwinked by the
powerful icons of the two-plus-two, gleaming-teeth
and never-a-row families of TV commercials.
David French, *head of the charity, Relate, alluding to
Princess Diana and the recent announcement of her
separation from Prince Charles, December 1992*

I think of my family as very special people.
We happen to be a very close-knit family.
Prince Charles

Now I suppose I'll be known as Charley's aunt.
Princess Margaret, *at the christening of Prince Charles*

FAT

Alvanley – who's your fat friend?
Beau Brummel, *of George IV, at the Cyprian's Ball, 1813*

But still there is unto a patriot nation,
    Which loves so well its country and its king,
A subject of sublimest exultation
    Bear it, ye Muses on your brightest wing!
Howe'er the mighty locust, Desolation
    Strip your green fields, and to your harvest
cling,
Gaunt famine never shall approach the throne –
Though Ireland starve, great George weighs twenty
stone.
Lord Byron *(1788-1824), English poet, of George IV,*
Don Juan *canto viii*

A corpulent Adonis of fifty.
James Leigh Hunt *(1784-1859), English poet and essayist,*
of George IV, in the Examiner, *1813*

FATE

Our hour is marked and no one can claim a moment
of life beyond what fate has predestined.
Napoleon I, *to Dr Arnot, April 1821*

For grief's afflictive bed uprose,
Great George resumes his sceptr'd sway;
As fate in pity to our woes,
Restor'd his intellectual day.
Anthony Pasquin *(John Williams), of George III,* An Ode
on His Majesty's Recovery

Let's talk of graves, of worms, and epitaphs;
Make dust our paper, and with rainy eyes
Write sorrow on the bosom of the earth . . .

For God's sake, let us sit down upon the ground,
and tell sad stories of the death of kings:
How some have been depos'd; some slain in war;
Some haunted by the ghosts they have depos'd;
Some poison'd by their wives; some sleeping kill'd;
All murder'd.
Richard II in Richard II, *by William Shakespeare*

After I am dead, the boy will ruin himself in twelve
months.
George V, *referring to his son, later to become King*
Edward VIII

FATHERHOOD

You know how much I was with your father, and
you are aware that it was he who placed the crown
of Egypt upon my head.
Cleopatra, *to Octavian, referring to Julius Caesar*

Kings are called Fathers of the fatherland, to show
them that they must be benevolent, not cruel.
Giambattista Cinthio Giraldi *(1504-73), Italian writer*

My father was frightened of his mother. I was
frightened of my father, and I'm damned well going
to make sure that my children are frightened of me.
George V

Prince George was fond of his sons but his manner
to them alternated between awkward jocularity of
the kind which makes a sensitive child squirm from
self-consciousness, and a severity bordering on
harshness.
Lady Airlie

*When Churchill, then Prime Minister, urged the Queen to
choose Windsor,* **Prince Philip** *was heard to cry*
'I'm just a bloody amoeba! That's all'.
   One of the Queen's private secretaries explains:
'I've always taken that to mean he was just there to
deposit semen.'

The Duke [of Edinburgh] was marvellous. He
always used to set aside time to read to the children
or put together those little model toys with them.
Princess Anne was very good at model making, but
not Prince Charles, he was all fingers and thumbs.
Mabel Anderson, *royal nanny, in Graham and Heather
Fisher*, Charles The Man and The Prince

FAULTS

We see men fall from high estate on account of the
very faults through which they attained it.
Jean de la Bruyère '*Of the Court*', Caractères, *1688*

Her chief fault (in little things and great) seems to be
impatience; in sea phrase, she always wants to go
ahead; she can't bear contradiction nor to be
thwarted.
Adolphus Fitzclarence, *of Queen Victoria, diary of
Charles Greville, 24 September 1842*

FAUX PAS

British women can't cook.
Prince Philip, *in a remark at the Scottish Women's Rural
Institute, 1986*

If you stay here much longer, you'll all be slitty eyed.
Prince Philip *to British students in Peking, 1986*

We don't come here for our health. We can think of
other ways of enjoying ourselves.
Prince Philip, *on a visit to Canada*

I have to be very careful when I look at a female. If I look more than once, they are immediately sized up as a future spouse. I imagine I shall have to be very careful on my trip north, especially with whom I rub noses.
Prince Charles, *on a trip to Canada. He later apologized for the remark, as some of Canada's Eskimos apparently took exception to it*

Is that a Cornish language?
Prince Charles, *on seeing a banner in the crowd which read* IE LIEK MIE KWEEN *while on a visit to the Isles of Scilly (part of the Duchy of Cornwall). He was told it was something called 'the initial teaching alphabet'*

A toast . . . to Prince Charles and Lady Jane.
Peter Balfour, *Chairman of the Scottish Council proposing a toast to Charles and his bride-to-be (Diana), 1981*

I'm sorry, love, but you can't come in here.
Eric Petherage, *gateman at Ascot, to Princess Anne, failing to recognise her and refusing her entry at the Sovereign's Gate*

You have so many people trooping past you all day that one person looks very much the same as the next. When I realised who it was I just wanted to sink into the ground and die.
Eric Petherage, *June 1993*

I . . . take Philip Charles Arthur George [instead of Charles Philip Arthur George] as my wedded husband.
Princess Diana, *at her wedding ceremony, 29 July 1981*

FAVOUR

The King cast a glancing eye towards him; which was easily observed by such as observed their Prince's humour . . . then one gave him his place of Cup bearer, that he might be in the King's eye; another sent to his Mercer and Taylor to put good clothes on him; a third to his Sempster for curious linen, and all as in – comes to obtain offices upon his future rise, then others took upon themselves to be his Braccoes, to undertake his quarrels upon affronts, put upon him by Somersets' Faction.

So all hands helped to the piecing up this new favourite.

Anthony Weldon (1648-1721), *referring to the First Duke of Buckingham*

FEAR

Fear not, we are of the nature of the lion, and cannot descend to the destruction of mice and such small beasts.

Elizabeth I, *to a lady of Queen Mary's household who had been cruel to her*

I don't know whether you realise how horrifying it is for an inexperienced person like myself to follow such a dazzling array of comedians. It is very, very difficult indeed and I have been worrying about it constantly for the last – well, for a week at least.

Prince Charles, *on being made an honorary member of the Grand Order of Water Rats*

I wish I could have found him before, as now that I know the right way to breathe, my fear of talking will vanish.

The Duke of York, *in a letter to his father (on finding a speech therapist who helped him cure his stammer), 1926*

FEMINISM

There will always be women's lib questions, and I can't remember what the required answer is when they're put to me. But, I don't force the models to do what they do.
Lord Patrick Lichfield, *photographer and cousin of Queen Elizabeth II, speaking at the launch of his fourteenth Unipart calender, featuring photographs of nude models, November 1992*

FEUD

He simply cannot see why no one shows any interest in his achievements and concentrates on her [Princess Diana] instead.
Courtier to Prince Charles to newsman talking on a Royal tour of Korea, October 1992, reported in Today, *January 1993*

FLATTERY

Everyone likes flattery; and when you come to Royalty you should lay it on with a trowel.
Benjamin Disraeli *(1804-81), British statesman and novelist*

Vulgarity in a King flatters the majority of the nation.
George Bernard Shaw

Though men in great positions are easily flattered, we are still more easily flattered, when in their company.
The Marquis de Vauvenargues *(1715-47), French moralist*, Reflections and Maxims *1746*

And lastly for our Royal guest,
A cheer from my wheezy chest;
Forgive my tendency to grovel
But he's just reviewed my latest novel.
Harry Secombe, *entertainer, paying tribute to Prince Charles who had reviewed his book for* Punch

FLIRTATION

Look after your Empire and I'll look after my life.
Princess Margaret, *accused by the Queen of flirting*

FOOD

Let them eat cake.
Marie Antoinette, *at the time of the French Revolution when her subjects were starving*

I have often seen the King consume four plates of different soups, a whole pheasant, a partridge, a large plate of salad, two big slices of ham, a dish of mutton in garlic sauce, a plateful of pastries followed by fruit and hard-boiled eggs. The King and Monsieur greatly like hard boiled eggs.
The Duchess of Orleans (1652-1722), *of her brother-in-law, Louis XIV, 1682*

I never see any home cooking. All I get is fancy stuff.
The Duke of Edinburgh, *on visiting a catering establishment*

None of the beef I have eaten at this age is edible.
Prince Philip, *at the Royal Dairy Show, 1965*

If it's got four legs and it's not a chair, if it's got two wings and it flies, but it's not an aeroplane, and if it swims and it's not a submarine, the Cantonese will eat it.
Prince Philip, *1986*

Horses and poets should be fed, not overfed.
Charles IX, *King of France (1550–74)*

Does Prince Philip shoot the pheasants himself? Or do they die of natural causes?
The Duke of Edinburgh's favourite press enquiry. The question is frequently asked when the Queen entertains and pheasant is on the menu

I'm constantly being asked to eat three-course meals
I don't really want.
Princess Anne, *launching her 'Skip Lunch, Save a Life'*
campaign and relieving official hosts from any obligation to
provide lavish refreshments, Slimmer *magazine, 1992*

He was a bold man who first swallowed an oyster.
James I and VI

Oh dear, I can't eat them because they're bad for my
hips.
The Duchess of York, on being offered chocolates by a child
while on a visit to a hospital in Zabrze, December 1992

FOREPLAY

Nell Gwyn, *mistress of Charles II, on discovering that a*
rival had been invited to the King's bed, entertained the
woman at a pre-coital dinner where she doctored her meal
with 'physical ingredients' . . .

The effect thereof had such an operation upon the
harlot, when the king was caressing her in bed with
the amorous sport of Venus, that a violent and
sudden looseness obliging her ladyship to discharge
her artillery, she made the King as well as herself in
a most lamentable pickle.
Reported by Alexander Smith in The School of Venus

FORGIVENESS

God may pardon you, but I never can.
Elizabeth I, *to the Countess of Nottingham*

I shall be an autocrat: that's my trade. And the good
Lord will forgive me: that's his.
Catherine the Great

FOUL

For nothing can seem foul to those that win.
King Henry, in Henry IV Part I by **William Shakespeare**

FREEDOM

The freedom of the press works in such a way that there is little freedom from it.
Princess Grace of Monaco *(1928-82)*

FRIENDS

Old friends are the best. King James used to call for his old shoes; they were easiest for his feet.
John Selden, *of James I and VI, (1584-1654), English historian and antiquary*, Table Talk

Except he became a protestant, his friends would be obliged to leave him, like a garrison one could no longer defend.
George Savile, *Marquis of Halifax, of James II*, Memoirs of Sir John Reresby

He has done a wonderful job helping me with all my financial work and has been a fantastic friend.
The Duchess of York, *replying to a question about her relationship with John Bryan*

I didn't say he was, I said he was a fantastic friend helping me with my financial work.
The Duchess of York, *replying to interviewer, Diane Sawyer, who suggested the American is not just a financial advisor*

She's downplaying him, but they are together. When visitors ask her if she is still with that ghastly American, she denies it. Then two minutes later someone will open a cupboard door and he'll be standing there.
Taki Theodoracopulos, *gossip columnist, May 1993*

GEORGES

George the First was always reckoned
Vile, but viler than George the Second;
And what mortal ever heard
Any good of George the Third?
When from earth the Fourth descended
God be praised the Georges ended.
Walter Savage Landor *(1775-1864), English writer*

GENTLEMAN

[Dr Johnson] said to Mr Barnard, 'Sir, they may talk
of the King as they will; but he is the finest
gentleman I have ever seen.' And he afterwards
observed to Mr Langton, 'Sir, his manners are those
of as fine a gentleman as we may suppose Louis the
Fourteenth or Charles the Second.'
James Boswell, *of George III*, Life of Johnson

A noble, hasty race he ran,
    Superbly filthy and fastidious;
He was the world's finest gentleman,
    And made the appellation hideous.
W.M. Praed *(1802-39), English man of letters, proposed
epitaph for George IV, 1825*

I can make a lord, but only God almighty can make
a gentleman.
James I and VI

GIFTS

Lady Di sent off a list of presents they'd like,
some fish forks, a toaster and a bike,
A cookbook, some plates, a potted dahlia,
And the head of a telephone engineer in Australia.
Spike Milligan, *part of a poem he wrote for the royal
couple (Prince Charles and Princess Diana), in celebration of
their marriage 1981*

83

Don't worry it's not Windsor Castle.
Official, presenting T-shirts depicting the ruined Tynemouth Priory to the Princess of Wales when she visited a drug abuse project in Whitley Bay

GLORY

By commanding so free and generous a nation, we make ourselves glorious.
Louis XIV, of France, at the beginning of his reign

GOD

Thus we have defeated the King of France at Gisors but it is not we who have done it, but God and our right through us.
Richard I

I am very sorry to know and hear how unreverently that most precious jewel, the word of God, is disputed, rhymed, sung and jangled in every ale-house and tavern, contrary to the true meaning and doctrine of the same.
Henry VIII (1491-1547), commenting on the translation of the Bible into English, Parliament, December 1545

I came, I saw. God conquered.
Charles V (1500-58), Holy Roman Emperor, after the battle of Muhlbert, April 1547

Spain: my God.
Alfonso XIII (1886-1941), King of Spain. The King went into exile in 1931 and never returned during his lifetime. Two weeks before he died he abdicated in favour of his third son

As for her own personal thoughts, I don't suppose she is telling anybody except God.
Lucy Murphy, spokeswoman for the Queen Mother, at the time of King George VI's death

How could God do this to me after all I have done
for him.
Louis XIV, *King of France, on receiving news of the French
army's defeat at the Battle of Blenheim*

GOOD

He was the worthyest gentleman, the best husbande,
the best father, and the best Christian, that the age
in which he lived had produced, and he was not the
best king, if he was without some parts and
qualityes which have made some kings great and
happy, no other Prince was ever unhappy, who was
possessed of half his virtues and indowments, and so
much without any kinde of vice.
Edward Hyde, *Earl of Clarendon (1609-74), English
statesman, of Charles I*

Could you but see how nobly he is bearing himself,
how wise he is, his love for all that is good and right,
and specially his love of learning, you would need
no wings to fly into the light of this new risen and
salutary star. Oh, Erasmus, could you but witness
the universal joy, could you but see how proud our
people are of their new sovereign, you would weep
for pleasure. Heaven smiles, earth triumphs and
flows with milk and honey and nectar. This king of
ours is no seeker after gold, or gems, or mines of
silver. He desires only the fame of virtue and eternal
life.
Lord Mountjoy, Letter to Easmus, *on the accession of Henry
VIII, translated by J.A. Froude*

I desire what is good, therefore everyone who does
not agree with me is a traitor.
George III

Charles the Second knew his people and rewarded
merit. The Church was at no time better filled than
in his reign. He was the best King we have had from
his time till the reign of his present Majesty, except
James the Second, who was a very good King.
Samuel Johnson, *James Boswells's* Life of Johnson

It is strange how everybody do nowadays reflect upon Oliver [Cromwell], and commend him, what brave things he did, and make all the neighbours fear him, while here a Prince, come in with all the love and prayer and good liking of his people . . . hath lost all so soon.
Samuel Pepys, *of Charles II,* Diary, *July 1677*

For the King himself, he seems all good nature and wishing to satisfy everybody; all his speeches are obliging. I saw him again yesterday, and was surprised to find the levee room had lost so entirely the air of the lion's den. This Sovereign don't stand in one spot, with his eyes fixed royally on the ground, and dropping bits of German news; he walks about and speaks to everybody. I saw him afterwards on the throne, where he is graceful and genteel, sits with dignity, and reads his answers to addresses well . . .
Horace Walpole, *of George III,* A.F. Scott, Every One a Witness, *1760*

She is a charming woman, an angel. There can be no doubt that her soul is as lovely as her face.
Napoleon I, *to his brother Lucien, of his mistress, Marie Walewska*

GOSSIP

A good gossip is a wonderful tonic.
The Queen

Better pointed bullets than pointed speeches.
Prince Otto von Bismarck

She'll wear the pants in that marriage.
Harvey Smith, *British showjumper, speaking of Princess Anne and her marriage to Mark Phillips*

The suggestion that they have been anything but supportive and sympathetic is untrue and particularly hurtful.
Princess Diana, *denying that the Queen and Prince Philip had cold-shouldered her after revelations about the problems of her marriage became public.*

The Princess of Wales would like to single out from the recent wave of misleading reports about the Royal family assertions in some newspapers this week directed specifically against the Queen and the Duke of Edinburgh.

Statement issued by the **Princess of Wales**, *7 November 1992*

GRIEF

Though it makes the unskilful laugh, cannot but make the judicious grieve.

Hamlet in Hamlet *by* **William Shakespeare**

I have full cause of weeping; but this heart
Shall break into a hundred thousand flaws
Or ere I'll weep.

Lear in King Lear *by* **William Shakespeare**

HABIT

Certainly she [Queen Mary] disliked untidiness in every form, even in plants that grew in a dishevelled manner and harboured dirt or dust: for this reason, among others, she was an inverterate and implacable foe to ivy, advising always that it should be cut down, and pulling it off walls herself and making others do so.

Sir Osbert Sitwell *(1892-1969), English author,* Queen Mary and Others, *1974*

HAPPINESS

Covetous only of a virtuous praise,
His life a lesson to the land he sways:
To touch the sword with conscientious awe,
Nor draw it but when duty bids him draw;
To sheathe it in the peace-restoring close
With joy beyond what victory bestows;
Blest country, where these kingly glories shine;
Blest England, if this happiness be thine!

William Cowper, *of George III*, Table Talk

HATE

Authority is never without hate.
Euripides *(480 or 484-406 BC), Greek dramatist, Ion,*
411 BC)

The Prince of Wales gives one the feeling of being
feeble and hating his position, none of the tact of his
father and they say obstinate.
Kathleen Isherwood, *of George V, Diary, 7 May 1910*

It makes one's flesh creep to think that such a man
should have been the ruler of millions . . . A prince
whose malignant cruelties made him loathed by his
contemporaries, and whose revolting predilections,
unless we ascribe them to a diseased brain, are not
only a slur on the age which tolerated them, but a
disgrace to the higher instincts of our common
nature.
Henry Buckle *(1821-62), English historian, of James II,*
History of Civilisation

All that stuff about sending her best wishes to Anne
for her wedding is rubbish. The two women hate
each other.
Palace insider, talking to the media, referring to the
relationship between Princess Diana and Princess Anne

HEALTH

Isn't it normal not to be able to cope all the time?
Isn't it normal for women as well as men to feel
frustrated with life? Isn't it normal to feel angry and
want to change a situation that is hurting?
    It could be a far more effective use of limited
resources to offer women the opportunity of
explaining their predicament sooner, rather than
wait until their strength to survive has been sapped.
Princess Diana, *in a speech to a conference on women and*
mental health, June 1993

With greater awareness and information, these people, who are locked into a spiral of secret despair, can be reached before the disease takes over their lives.
Princess Diana, *on bulimia, May 1993*

The reason the Queen Mother isn't gaga is that she uses her brain.
Dame Barbara Cartland

The word spiritual can make people cringe. Notebooks are shut and eyes turn to the skies.
The Princess of Wales, *on the merits of spiritual healing*

HEART

When I am dead and opened, you shall find 'Calais' lying in my heart.
Mary Tudor *(1516-53)*

HEIR

. . . The heir, as long as he is a child, differeth nothing from a servant.
Galatians 4.1

HERO

They tell me the fire is contained. I was down there in the Mews doing research for the Staff College when I heard the alarm. I went straight up to see what I could do. There was no panic and no fuss because everybody did their job. The worst thing was the smoke.
Prince Andrew, *talking to television reporters about the Windsor castle fire, November 1992. He was among the first on the scene, and helped get furniture and paintings out*

89

HINDSIGHT

His views and affections were singly confined to the narrow compass of the Electorate: England was too big for him.
Lord Chesterfield *(1694-1773), of George I*

. . . this haughty, vigilant, resolute, sagacious blue-stocking, half Mithridates and half Trissotin, bearing up against a world in arms.
T.B. Macaulay, *of Frederick the Great*

HISTORY

History will, I believe, show that communism was a phenomenon which, though it might have been born of idealism and a sense of injustice, in practice betrayed the very people it was alleged to serve.
The Queen, *speaking in Hungary, May 1993*

HOBBIES

He is all right as a gay young midshipman. He may be all right as a wise old King. But the intervening period when he was Duke of York just shooting at Sandringham, is hard to manage or swallow. For seventeen years he did nothing at all but kill animals and stick in stamps.
Harold Nicolson *(1886-1968), English diplomat, author and critic, of George V,* Diary, *17 August 1949*

HOLIDAYS

We've never had a holiday. A week or two at Balmoral or ten days at Sandringham is the nearest we get.
Princess Anne, *British Airways in-flight magazine* High Life, *1976*

HOME

We live in what virtually amounts to a museum –
which does not happen to a lot of people.
Prince Philip, *of Windsor Castle*

There's nowhere for the Queen to stay tonight, so
she will be returning to Buckingham Palace.
Prince Andrew, *talking after the Windsor Castle fire*, Daily
Mirror, *21 November 1992*

Windsor is a home, a family home, whereas
Buckingham Palace is really only an office.
Prince Edward, Daily Mail, *November 1992*

You will be home before the leaves have fallen from
the trees.
Wilhelm II, *to troops leaving for the front, August 1914*

HONOUR

Do therefore, when thou art come to Jerusalem,
send for the leading men among them and show
them my body, and with great appearance of
sincerity give them leave to use it as they themselves
please, whether they will dishonour the dead body
by refusing it burial, as having severely suffered by
my means, or whether in their anger they will offer
any other injury to that body. Promise them also
that thou wilt do nothing without them in the affairs
of the Kingdom. If thou dost but say this to them, I
shall have the honour of a more glorious funeral
from them, than thou could'st have made for me:
and when it is within their power to abuse my dead
body, they will do it no injury at all, and thou wilt
rule in safety.
Alexander, *King of Judea, to his wife (d. 145 BC)*

HUMAN

British management doesn't seem to understand the importance of the human factor.
Prince Charles, *speaking at the Parliamentary and Scientific Committee lunch, February 1979*

Those who see and observe kings, heroes and statesmen, discover that they have headaches, indigestion, humours and passions, just like other people; every one of which in their turns determine their wills in defiance of their reason.
Lord Chesterfield, *to his son, 5 December 1749*

Great though they are, Kings are only human.
Pierre Corneille *(1606-84), French dramatist,* Le Cid

HUMOUR

Good morning, gentlemen both.
Elizabeth I, *addressing a group of tailors,* Sayings of Queen Elizabeth, *Chamberlain*

I have known many persons who turned their gold into smoke, but you are the first to turn smoke into gold.
Elizabeth I, *to Sir Walter Raleigh, on his introduction of tobacco into England*

Mad is he? then I hope he will bite some of my other generals.
George II *(1683-1760), replying to the Duke of Newcastle who complained that General Wolfe was a madman,* The Life and Letters of James Wolfe, *Wilson*

Prince Charles is planning to record his own version of Frank Sinatra's hit, *My Way*. He's going to call it *One Did it One's Way.*
Neil Shand

I hope it's the right size.
Prince Charles, *on tour in New Zealand, after being presented with a matrimonial ball and chain, 1981*

Of course, haggis live in Scotland, have only three legs and can only go around one side of a hill.
Prince Charles, *addressing an environmental conference, and noticing that haggis was on the menu*

I've been told Princess Di and Prince Charles are going to get a separation. And the palace is saying that Charles is seeking custody of the plants.
Joan Rivers, *American talk-show host and comedienne, 1992*

The prospect of finding ways of amusing and entertaining such a vast and hideously professional gallery of show-business personalities has led me for the first time in my life to seek the services of a ghost-writer. Such ethereal creatures are hard to locate, but with the help of the Metropolitan Police ghost squad and Jimmy Edwards's agent – who offered to be my agent, I may tell you – some of you must know him – a suitably spectral author was tracked down in one of the more salubrious quarters of London. Upon investigation, his terms seemed surprisingly reasonable – one hair from the head of each of my many girl-friends, a cup of Metropolitan Police tea, the tail of a Grand Water Rat and a pair of my pyjamas now on loan to *Woman's Own*.*
Prince Charles, *on being made a honorary member of the Grand Order of Water Rats.*
(**Interviewed on behalf of the magazine, Charles had been asked whether or not he wore pyjamas in bed. He declined to answer*)

Ah, I thought there was one fewer around when I came down to breakfast this morning.
Prince Charles, *at the Water Rats' lunch, on seeing the menu, written in Welsh, with not-too-serious translations – the first course being Cold Broth of Corgi*

I hear that in America, they spray so much insecticide around that even the cannibals have begun to complain that Americans taste of DDT.
Prince Charles, *in a speech at the Cambridge Union*

Ah, I thought I passed a grin coming in.
Prince Charles, *at Welbeck colliery, speaking to a miner, who told the Prince that he had dropped his false teeth on the conveyor belt and had been unable to retrieve them*

The most important thing a person in my position can have is a sense of humour . . . being able to laugh at oneself.
Prince Charles

Were it not for my ability to see the funny side of my life, I would have been committed to an institution long ago.
Prince Charles

The oldest profession in the world.
Prince Charles, *referring to the monarchy*

I'm one of their most devoted and dotty supporters.
Prince Charles, *referring to the Goons and speaking as their honorary public relations officer*

. . . Then I discovered the *Ying Tong Song* in record form and almost at once I knew it by heart – the only song I do know by heart. I plagued everybody with its dulcet dones and *Solo for Raspberry Blower* to such an extent that when my small brothers heard a recording of the Goons for the first time, they thought it was their elder brother.
Prince Charles, *prefacing a Christmas volume of Goon show scripts, 1973*

HUSBANDS

He never laughs at my jokes.
Princess Diana, *referring to her husband*

We know all about that. She's not far wrong.
Princess Diana, *in response to Dr Miriam Stoppard's statement that marriage is bad for women, and living with a man constitutes a health hazard which should carry a government warning*

I'm referred to in that splendid language [Urdu] as 'Fella belong Mrs Queen'.
Prince Philip, *on a Royal tour of India*

He was a born salesman. He would be an admirable representative of Rolls-Royce. But an ex-King cannot start selling motor cars.
The Duchess of Windsor, *referring to her husband*

I think that everyone will concede that – today of all days – I should begin by saying, 'My Husband and I'.
The Queen, *on her Silver Wedding, in a speech at the Guildhall, 1972*

Celibacy is the better stake, since the best husband is not worth a fig.
The Duchess of Orleans

The King has been very good to me. He promoted me from a simple maid to be a marchioness. Then he raised me to be a Queen. Now he will raise me to be a martyr.
Anne Boleyn

HYPOCRISY

I'm delighted Lord McGregor's letter has come to light. It might make one or two hypocrites think differently. There are many politicians and others in the establishment who wish to blame the press for everything.

David Chipp, *former Editor in Chief of the Press Association, welcoming the news that the name of the press had been cleared over the press coverage of Royal events*

IDEAS

If anyone has a new idea in this country, there are twice as many people who advocate putting a man with a red flag in front of it.

Prince Philip

IMPATIENCE

I almost had to wait.

Louis XIV, *attrib., when a coach he had ordered arrived just in time*

An impatient girl . . . She has a 35-25-37 figure and likes to display to good advantage the maximum amount of leg.

A description of Princess Anne while on tour in America, the New York Sunday Post, *1970*

IMPORTANCE

On the first Australian tour the Queen and Prince Philip made, he was introducd to a Mr and Mrs Robinson. Mr Robinson explained that his wife was a Doctor of Philosophy – 'very much more important than me,' he explained. 'Ah yes,' said the Duke, 'we have that trouble in our family too.'

IMPRESSIONS

Harris, I am not well, pray get me a glass of brandy.
George IV, *on seeing Caroline of Brunswick, his future wife, for the first time, diary of the Earl of Malmsbury*

As just and merciful as Nero and as good a Christian as Mohammed.
John Wesley *(1703-91), British religious leader, of Elizabeth I, Journal, April 1768*

The mere scum of the earth.
The Duke of Wellington, *on his men*

Of all the bulls that live, this hath the greatest asses ears.
Elizabeth I, *attrib., of the composer, John Bull*

A silk stocking filled with mud.
Napoleon I's *description of the French statesman, Talleyrand*

A dull, stupid and profligate King, full of drink and low conversation, without dignity of appearance or manner, without sympathy of any kind with the English people and the English ways, and without the slightest knowledge of the English language.
Justin McCarthy, *of George I*

He (George II) had the haughtiness of Henry VIII without his spirit; the avarice of Henry VII, without his exactions; the indignities of Charles I without his bigotry for his prerogative the vexation of King William, with as little skill in the management of parties; and the gross gallantry of his father, without his good nature or his honesty: he might perhaps, have been honest, if he had never hated his father, or had ever loved his son.
Horace Walpole, *Memoirs*

As I was going by Charing Cross,
I saw a black man upon a black horse;
They told me it was King Charles the First –
Oh dear, my heart was ready to burst.
Nursery rhyme, traditional

His makims, in mid-career, were those of a conscientious bull in a china shop.
Richard Pares, George III and the Politicians

The loathsome Lackwit, James I
Samuel Taylor Coleridge (1772-1834), *English poet*, Notebook

Under the morose face there seemed to be a heart of stone.
Alexander Smellie, *of James II*, Men of the Covenant

. . . A young woman of noted independence. She made no effort to conceal a mood of incredulity and vague discomfort.
New York Times, *of Princess Anne on tour with Prince Charles as guests of President Nixon in Washington*, 1970

The Prince is full of pep, the Princess acts pooped.
Washington Daily News, *referring to Prince Charles and Princess Anne on American tour*, 1970

INCOMPETENCE

Our dear King James is good and honest, but the most incompetent man I have ever seen in my life. A child of seven years would not make such silly mistakes as he does.
The Duchess of Orleans, *referring to James II who was in exile in France, letter to the Electress Sophia, 6 June 1692*

INDEPENDENCE

I was the last to consent to the separation; but the separation having been made . . the first to meet the friendship of the United States as an independent power.
George III, *in an address to John Adams, the first American envoy to Britain, 1776*

INDULGENCES

What grimaces, what capers, leaps and chuckles
prime ministers, presidents and kings must indulge
in, in the privacy of their bedrooms, so as to avenge
their systems of the daylong strain imposed on
them!
Paul Valéry *(1871-1945), French poet and writer,* Tel
Quel, *1941-43*

INDUSTRY

In the days when the nation depended on agriculture
for its wealth it made the Lord Chancellor sit on a
woolsack to remind him where the wealth came
from. I would like to suggest we move that now and
make him sit on a crate of machine tools.
Prince Philip, *'Sayings of the Week'*, Observer, *10 October
1982*

It may not have been the case that industry was
actually despised, but that members of the Royal
House had not found a way to intimacy of touch
with it . . . the wisest influences in the ranks of
industry are nowadays turned to the cultivation of
pride in work well done rather than to shame of an
overall and grimy hands. And the Duke [of York] is
taking his part in this task.
The Yorkshire Post, *1928*

INFIDELITY

If fate had given me in my youth a husband whom I
could have loved, I should have remained always
true to him. The trouble is that my heart would not
willingly remain one hour without love.
Catherine the Great, *letter to Prince Potemkin, 1774*

Have you ever stopped to think that for the last 40 years, I have never moved anywhere without a policeman accompanying me? So how the *hell* could I get away with anything like that?
Prince Philip, *in response to questions about rumours of his infidelity, December 1992*

I just don't think he's at all sexual in that way. He gets it all out playing polo, or sailing, or working. But not that. It's just not him.
A Royal Courtier, defending Prince Philip and dispelling rumours of his infidelity

Prince Charles and Camilla are a very tactile couple – always touching and brushing against one another. It was embarrassing for staff to witness.
Anonymous butler of the royal household, in a newspaper interview, referring to the relationship between Prince Charles and Camilla Parker-Bowles

I demonstrated with some warmth that there was only one blackguard in this case.
Lord Charles Beresford, *12 January 1890. It was said at the time that Lord Charles, angered by the behaviour towards his wife of the Prince of Wales [Bertie] actually struck the heir to the throne, but more reliably that he pushed up against him causing him to sit down suddenly upon a sofa*

INNOCENCE

One can't reign and be innocent.
Louis Antoine Léon de Saint-Just (1767-94), *French revolutionary*, Discours à la convention, *13 November 1792*

INTELLIGENCE

Nowadays a parlourmaid as ignorant as Queen Victoria was when she came to the throne would be classed as mentally defective.
George Bernard Shaw

Now remember everything rests with you, and you are quite intelligent and can do well if you like.
George V, to Prince Albert while a naval cadet at Osborne, 1910

INTENTIONS

For the best intentioned of great men need a few scoundrels around them; there are some things you cannot ask an honest man to do.
Jean de la Bruyère, Caractères, 1688

Princes had need, in tender matters and ticklish times to beware what they say: especially in these short speeches, which fly abroad like darts, and are thought to be shot out of their secret intentions.
Sir Francis Bacon (1561-1626), *English philosopher and statesman, 'Of Sedition and Troubles', Essays, 1597-1625*

INTRODUCTIONS

But you told me to be on my best behaviour to his Royal Highness. I showed him the best I have, and it was free.
La Barucci, *who called herself the greatest whore in the world, after being introduced to the young Prince of Wales, c. 1860. She had been briefed to be on her best behaviour, but as she curtsied, she dropped her clothes to the floor*

INVESTITURE

Your friends will understand that as a Prince you are obliged to do things which may seem a little silly.
Queen Mary, to her son Edward, Prince of Wales, before his investiture at Caernarvon, 1911

Today bells ring, bands play, flags are unfurled,
Anxieties and feuds lie buried
Under a ceremonial joy. You sir, inherit
A weight of history in a changing world,
Its treasured wisdom and its true
Aspirings the best birthday gift for you.
Cecil Day-Lewis (1904-72), *poet laureate, first verse of a poem to celebrate the investiture of Prince Charles as Prince of Wales, 1969*

JEALOUSY

Love engenders jealousy, but jealousy kills love.
Christina of Sweden

JUDGEMENT

I have long since been aware that your King is a man of the greatest honour and bravery, but he is imprudent.
Saladin, *Sultan of Egypt and Syria (1137-93), referring to Richard I, to the Bishop of Salisbury, 1192*

I perceive that that man hath the sow by the right ear.
Henry VII (1491-1547), *in a letter to his mother, referring to Cranmer, an English churchman*

This judgement I have of you, that you will not be corrupted with any manner of gift and that you will be faithful, you will give me that counsel that you think best.
Elizabeth I, *to William Cecil, 1558*

JUSTICE

Who but my father would keep such a bird in a cage?
Henry, *Prince of Wales referring to Sir Walter Raleigh, who was imprisoned in the Tower of London for treason in 1603*

An emperor is subject to no one but God and
Justice.
Frederick I *(Barbarossa) (1122-90)*, Apopthegmata,
Book 1, Julius Wilhelm Zincgref, 1626

King James was not the first prince who loved
justice, hated iniquity and died in exile; yet there
never was perhaps, any ruler of any country, who in
his lifetime suffered so much from the disloyalty of
his own family, and the ingratitude of his friends,
and after his death, from the injustice of posterity.
Malcolm V. Hay, Enigma of James II

KINGDOMS

Kingdoms are but cares,
State is devoid of stay;
Riches are ready snares,
and hasten to decay.
Henry VI *(1421-71)*, Nugae Antiques, *Sir John Harrington,*
1769

The use of the sea and air is common to all; neither
can a title to the ocean belong to any people or
private persons, forasmuch as neither nature nor
public use and custom permit any possession
thereof.
Elizabeth I, *to the Spanish Ambassador, 1580*

It is upon the navy under the Providence of God that
the safety, honour and welfare of this realm do
chiefly attend.
Charles II, Articles of War, *1652 (Preamble)*

KINGS

You had better have one King than five hundred.
Charles II, *after dissolving the Oxford Parliament, March*
1681

George, be a King.
Augusta of Saxe-Gothe, *Princess of Wales (1719-72),*
mother of King George III

There will soon be only five kings left – the kings of England, Diamonds, Hearts, Spades and Clubs.
Farouk I (1902-65), *the last King of Egypt, in a remark made to Lord Boyd-Orr*

A king is a thing men have made for their own sakes, for quietness' sake. Just as if in a family one man is appointed to buy the meat.
John Selden (1584-1654), *English jurist and statesman*

Don't forget your great guns, which are the most respectable arguments of the rights of kings.
Frederick the Great

Divine right of kings means the divine right of anyone who can get uppermost.
Herbert Spencer (1820-1903), *English philosopher*

Rigorous authority and justice are the kindness of kings.
Napoleon I, Maxims, *1804-15*

A king nowadays is no more than a hitchin post f'r wan pollytician afther another. He ain't allowed to move himself, but anny crazy pollytician that ties up to him is apt to pull him out be th' roots.
Finley Peter Dunne (1867-1936), *American humourist*, 'King Edward's Coronation', Observations by Mr Dooley, 1902

A king can stand people's fighting but he can't last long if people start thinking.
Will Rogers (1879-1935), *US actor and humourist*, 'The Autobiography of Will Rogers', 1949

Kings stands more in need of company of the intelligent than the intelligent do of the society of kings.
S.A. and D.I. Gulistant (1258), *tr. James Ross*

A king is he who has laid fear aside and the base longings of an evil heart; whom ambition unrestrained and the fickle favour of the reckless mob move.
Seneca (c. 5BC–AD65), *Roman philosopher and statesman*, Thyestes

Not all the water in the rough rude sea
Can wash the balm from an anointed king.
King Richard in Richard II *by* **William Shakespeare**

All kings are mostly rapscallions.
Mark Twain *(pseudonym of Samuel Longhorn Clemens, 1835-1910), American writer,* The Adventures of Huckleberry Finn, *1884*

The first who was king was a fortunate soldier.
Voltaire *(1694-1778), French author,* Merope, *1743*

Better to rely on one powerful King than on many little princes.
Jean de La Fontaine, Le Bassa et le Marchand

You would probably find it easier to choose a child fit to govern a country and to make a great King, than to discover a great violin.
Denis Diderot *(1713-84), French writer*

There is nothing kings like more than prompt obedience, and nothing that pleases them less than discovering obstacles.
Jean Baptiste Poquelin Molière *(1622-73), French playwright*

A king is never beholden to his subjects.
Pierre Corneille *(1606-84), French dramatist*

A Glorious Prince this Parliament
    The King should be, did swear,
But now we understand they meant
    In heaven and not here.

King and no King was once a play
    Or table on the stage
But see! It is become this day
    The moral of our age.
Marchamont Nedham, *of Charles I,* A Short History of the English Rebellion Compiled in Verse

So have I seen a King at chess
    (His rooks and knights withdrawn)
His queen and bishops in distress
(Shifting about grow less and less)
    With here and there a pawn.
Charles Sackville, *Earl of Dorset (1603-1706), of Charles II*, On the Young Statesmen

Kings are not born; they are made by artificial hallucination. When the process is interrupted by adversity at a critical age, as in the case of Charles II, the subject becomes sane and never completely recovers his kingliness.
George Bernard Shaw, '*Maxims for Revolutionists' in* Man and Superman

So much unaffected good nature and propriety appears in all he says and does that it cannot but endear him to all; but whether anything can long endear a King, or an angel in this strange factious country I cannot tell. I have the best opinion imaginable of him; not from anything he does or says just now, but because I have a moral certainty that he was in his nursery the honestest, most true and good-natured child that ever lived . . . What the child was, the man most certainly is, in spite of temporary appearances.
Lady Hervey, *of George III, Alan Lloyd*, The Wickedest Age

He was born a King, and from that height, the less fitted to look into inferior things; yet few escaped his knowledge, being, as it were, a magazine to retain them.
Arthur Wilson, *of James I*, The History of Great Britain

He would have been an excellent King of Spain.
Charles Whibley, *of James I*, George Jeffreys

Henry V was not the bluff patriot king of Shakespeare's plays; he was a dour and martial fanatic, obsessed by religion and his legal rights.
John Bowle, *England a Portrait*

KISSING

A young woman who allows herself to be kissed and caressed goes the rest of the way too.
The Duchess of Orleans

Whoever wins or loses the match, the Prince is bound to get a kiss from the Princess.
Aide to Prince Charles in a comment to the press before a polo match in Jaipur. The prince was playing and Diana was handing out the prizes. After the match, Charles received his prize, but no kiss. February 1992

KNOWLEDGE

A great man ought never to pry too minutely into things, least of all in unpleasant matters. For though it is important to know all, it is not necessary to know all about all.
Grecian, The Art of Worldly Wisdom, *1647*

O that I were as great
As is my grief, or lesser than my name!
Or that I could forget what I have been!
Or not remember what I must be now!
Richard II, in Richard II *by* **William Shakespeare**

LAND

We will give him seven feet of English ground or as much more as he may be taller than other men.
Harold II (1022-66), *immediately before the Norman Conquest, 1066*

By the splendour of God I have taken possession of my realm, the earth of England is in my two hands.
William the Conqueror (1027-87), *after falling over when coming ashore at Pevensey with his army of invasion*

Henceforth Prussia merges into Germany.
Frederick William IV, *King of Prussia (1795-1861), March 1848*

LANGUAGE

I speak Spanish to God, Italian to women, French to men, and German to my horse.
Charles V, *Holy Roman Emperor*

If anything, I've thought of myself as Scandinavian. Particularly Danish. We spoke English at home. The others learned Greek. I could understand a certain amount of it. But then the [conversation] would go into French, then it went into German, on occasion, because we had German cousins. If you couldn't think of a word in one language, you tended to go off in another.
Prince Philip, *December 1992*

LIFE

Of all I had, only honour and life have been spared.
Francis I, *King of France (1494-1547) referring to his defeat and capture by the forces of the Emperor Charles V at the Battle of Bavia, 1525*

1992 is not a year on which I shall look back with undiluted pleasure. In the words of one of my more sympathetic correspondents it has turned out to be an *annus horribilis*.
The Queen, *speaking at a banquet in London's Guildhall to mark her 40th year on the throne, November 1992*

Throughout the greater part of his life George III was a king of consecrated obstruction.
Walter Bagehot *(1826-77), English economist and journalist, The English Constitution*

George the Third
Ought never to have occurred.
One can only wonder
At so grotesque a blunder.
E.C. Bentley, Biography for Beginners

The life of the King is moving slowly to its close.
George V, *BBC radio news bulletin, Henry Channon, Diary, 20 January 1936*

Everything is going nowadays. Before long, I shall also have to go.
George VI, in conversation with Vita Sackville-West, February 1948, Harold Nicolson, Diary

Methinks it's as pretty an honest, drinking, whoring age as man would wish to live in.
Thomas Shadwell (c. 1642-92), English dramatist, summing up London in the time of Charles II, The Sullen Lovers

LOVE

I have never loved anyone for love's sake, except, perhaps, Josephine – a little.
Napoleon I

Though God hath raised me high, yet this I count the glory of my crown: that I have reigned with your love.
Elizabeth I, to a deputation from the House of Commons, November 1601

Life is too short to be able to love as one should.
Christina of Sweden

The trouble is that my heart is loath to remain even one hour without love . . . Let the mind rest in order that the feelings should be free.
Catherine the Great, to Prince Potemkin

The subject of love is the King's best guard.
Dr Thomas Fuller (1608-61), English historian, Gnomologia, 1732

He who loves me, let him follow me.
Philip VI (Prince of Valois) (1293-1350), attrib.

There are too many reasons why I love Sarah. I love her, that's the end of the story.
Prince Andrew, speaking of the Duchess of York, 18 August 1990

One day the children will fly the nest and Andrew and I will be there together.
Duchess of York, 18 August 1990

Better lo'ed ye canna be,
Will ye no come back again?
Caroline Nairne *(1766-1845), Scottish songwriter,*
referring to Bonnie Prince Charlie, from the song, Charlie is
my Darling.

If love prevailed with him more than any other
passion, he had this for excuse, besides that his
complexion was of an amorous sort, the women
seemed to be the aggressors; and I have since heard
the king say that they would sometimes offer
themselves to his embrace . . .
Sir John Reresby, *of James II,* Memoirs

As no other reason appeared in favour of their
choice but handsomeness, so the love the King
showed was as amorously conveyed as if he had
mistaken their sex, and thought them ladies; which I
have seen Somerset and Buckingham labour to
resemble in the effeminateness of their dressings.
Francis Osborn, *of James I's interest in young men*

They are very happy together. He is a very nice guy
and is totally committed to the marriage. And
having made a false start with Mark she will not
make the same mistake again.
Royal source referring to Princess Anne and Commander
Tim Laurence

Whatever happens I will always love you.
Remark said to have been made by **Prince Charles** *to*
Camilla Parker Bowles in a telephone conversation,
overheard by Princess Diana, June 1992

He doesn't wear his heart on his sleeve. I always
wanted to see him put his arm around the Queen
[Elizabeth II], and show her how much he adored
her, what you'd do for any wife. But he always sort
of stood to atention. I mentioned it to him a couple
of times. But he just gave me a hell of a look.
Michael Parker, *of Prince Philip. Parker worked for the*
Prince for many years

He [Charles II] thought no man sincere, nor woman honest, out of principle; but that whenever they proved so, humour or vanity was at the bottom of it. No one, he fancied, served him out of love, and therefore he endeavoured to be quits with the world by loving others as little as he thought they loved him.
Gilbert Burnet

The amours of a good King are always deemed a pardonable weakness, proving they are not attended with injustice or violence.
Niccolò Machiavelli *(1469-1526), Italian statesman*

[Prince Philip] was the man with whom Princess Elizabeth had been in love from their first meeting.
Sir John Wheeler-Bennett, *Royal biographer*

I suppose one thing led to another. I suppose I began to think about it seriously, oh, let me think now, when I got back in forty-six [1946] and went to Balmoral.
Prince Philip, *speaking of his attraction to Princess Elizabeth*

Your Majesties are more beloved by all classes and conditions, than any of the princes of the past.
Winston Churchill *(1874-1965), in a letter to King George VI*

The Queen was superb. She really does manage to convey to each individual in the crowd that he or she has had a personal greeting. But she is in truth one of the most amazing Queens since Cleopatra.
Harold Nicolson, *Royal commentator, referring to Queen Elizabeth, now the Queen Mother, 1939*

She was in her best mood and spirits. She has that astonishing gift of being sincerely interested in dull people, and dull occasions. Really, the woodwork, the pottery and the drawings with which Morley students occupy themselves in the evening are horrible objects. But the Queen Mother seemed really interested and spoke to almost all of them.
Harold Nicolson, *of the Queen Mother's visit to Morley College, 1958*

LOVE IS . . .

*The following is an account of a televised interview
with Charles and Diana following the
announcement of their engagement:*

Their first meeting?
In the middle of a ploughed field.
Diana

The proposal?
I wanted to give her a chance to think about it – to
think if it was all going to be too awful.
Charles. *(Diana had flown to Australia for a holiday before
the engagement become public)*

Shared interests?
Love of outdoors, skiing.
Charles

Music and dancing, and we both have the same
sense of humour. But I don't ride. I fell off a horse
and lost my nerve.
Diana

The age gap?
I haven't really thought about it.
Diana

Diana will help me stay young.
Charles

Her future as the Princess of Wales?
She will be 20 soon and I was about that age when I
started. It's difficult to start with, but you just have
to plunge in.
Charles

With Charles beside me, it can't go wrong.
Diana

LOVE LETTERS

I am so anxious for you not to abdicate and I think the fact that you do is going to put me me in the wrong light to the entire world because they will say that I could have prevented it.
Wallis Simpson, *to Edward VIII*

LOVERS

Marry your lover, it's the only way to regain your liberty.
Princess Mathilde *(1820-1904)*

Gaius Octavius had a desire to have reserved Cleopatra as a captive to adorn his Triumph, therefore he sent for the Psylli, a people whose faculty and employment is to suck out poison and he made them apply themselves to her wounds, to see if they could draw forth that venom which her asps had her death. He did Anthony and Cleopatra that favour as to be finished which was begun by themselves.
Suetonius, Lives of the Caesars

My wife is not Prince Charles's lover. It is not true. It is what I said last time, it's fiction.
Andrew Parker-Bowles, *denying rumours of a romantic relationship between his wife, Camilla, and Prince Charles,* Today, *November 1992*

Shall the dog lie where the deer once crouched?
Nell Gwyn, *refusing a lover after the King's death*

LUCK

The King was heard to say in the drawing room upon the falling of the South Sea Stock: 'We had very good luck; for we sold out last week!'
Joseph Spence *(1699-1768), English anecdotist, of George I,* Anecdotes

MADNESS

His madness can be best explained as the breakdown of too costly a struggle to maintain this artificial character – the reserve and equanimity imposed upon a hot temper and anxious nerves, to say nothing of this resolute fidelity to a hideous queen, and a regimen of violent and exaggerated abstinence designed to counteract strong passions and a tendency to fat.
Richard Pares, George III and the Politicians

He made me mad
To see him shine so brisk, and smell so sweet,
And talk so like a waiting gentlewoman
Of guns, and drums, and wounds God save the mark!
And telling me the sovereignest thing on earth
Was parmeceti for an inward bruise.
Hotspur in Henry IV, Part I *by* **William Shakespeare**

The whole family goes out in weather most would think mad.
Mabel Anderson, *referring to the Royal family's participation in field sports even in the severest winter conditions*

MALAPROPISMS

Those damned Pavarottis.
Description of waiting paparazzi, by a senior policeman at the wedding of Princess Anne to Commander Tim Laurence, December, 1992

MANAGEMENT

British management doesn't seem to understand the importance of the human factor.
Prince Charles, *in a speech to the Parliamentary and Scientific Committee, 21 February 1979*

The trouble with senior management, I notice as an outsider, is that there are too many one-ulcer men holding down two-ulcer men's jobs.
Prince Philip, Handbook of 20th-Century Quotations

MARRIAGE

I feel sure that no girl could go to the altar, and would probably refuse, if she knew all.
Queen Victoria

Of course I do have a slight advantage over the rest of you. It helps in a pinch to be able to remind your bride that you gave up a throne for her.
The Duke of Windsor, *previously Edward VIII*

So I went in with both feet and said, this is going to work and went to fly my helicopters and fly my airplanes. One thing I might say is to make sure you spend a long time before you make your decision and really know your man.
The Duchess of York, *in an interview on American television, December 1992*

Marriage is a sovereign remedy against love.
Christina of Sweden

I would rather be a beggar and single, than Queen and married . . . I should call the wedding-ring the yoke-ring.
Elizabeth I

If I'd ever married him, I'd have had to crack his head open to find out if there was anything in it.
Princess Mathilde, *on her cousin, Louis Napoleon*

Wednesday, July 29th
ROYAL WEDDING DAY!!!!
. . . Prince Charles looked quite handsome in spite
of his ears. His brother is dead good looking; it's a
shame they couldn't have swapped heads just for the
day.
Sue Townsend, The Secret Diary of Adrian Mole,
Aged 13¾, *1982*

My Lord [Sandwich] . . . telling me the story of how
the Duke of York hath got my Lord Chancellor's
daughter with child, and that she doth lay it to him,
and that for certain he did promise her marriage,
and had signed it with his blood, but that he by
stealth had got the paper out of her Cabinet. And
that the King would have him marry her, but that he
would not. So that the thing is very bad for the Duke
and for them all. But my Lord doth make light of it,
as a thing that he believes is not a new thing to the
Duke to go abroad. Discoursing concerning what if
the Duke should marry her, my Lord told me that
among his father's many old sayings that he had
writ in a book of his, this is one: . . . that he doth get
a wench with child, and married her afterward it is
as if a man should shit in his hat and then clap it
upon his head.
Samuel Pepys, *of James II,* Diary, *7 October 1660*

You have to remember when you marry in my
position that you're going to marry someone who,
perhaps one day, is going to be queen . . . The one
advantage about marrying a princess, for instance,
or someone from a royal family is that they do know
what happens.
Prince Charles, *July 1982*

Married life is wonderful.
Prince Andrew, *November 1986*

Basically, I feel a mixture of elation and terror –
which certainly gets me out of bed in the morning.
Viscount Linley, *on the prospect of his marriage to Serena
Stanhope,* Mail on Sunday, *May 1993*

A princely marriage is the brilliant addition of a
universal fact, and as such it rivets mankind.
Walter Bagehot, The English Constitution

Whatever your place in life. When you marry you
are forming a partnership you hope will last for fifty
years. So I would want to marry someone whose
interests I could share.
Prince Charles, *philosophising on the subject of marriage
(before meeting his future wife)*

Totally compatible.
Lady Sarah McCorquodale *(sister of Diana), describing
Prince Charles and Diana before their marriage*

The only trouble is that I often feel I would like to
marry somebody English. Or Welsh. Well British
anyway.
Prince Charles, *in reply to a question about who he should
marry*

You will find that people tend to marry within their
own circles. The advantage perhaps is that there is a
certain built-in acceptance of the sort of life you are
going to lead.
Prince Philip, *in an American TV interview about royal
marriages*

MEDICINE

The whole imposing edifice of modern medicine is
like the celebrated tower of Pisa – slightly off
balance.
Prince Charles

MEMORIES

He loved to talk over all the stories of his life to every man that came about him . . . He went over these in a very graceful manner, but so often and so copiously that all those who had been long accustomed to them grew weary of them; And when he entered on those stories they usually withdrew: So that he often began them in a full audience, and before he had done there were not above four or five left about him.
Gilbert Burnet, *of Charles II*

MEN

When a man says he approves of something in principle, it means he hasn't the slightest intention of putting it into practice.
Prince Otto von Bismarck

One should be more afraid of a stupid man than of an evil one.
Christina of Sweden

One man with a head on his shoulders is worth a dozen without.
Elizabeth I

Man is not made for pleasure, but pleasure for man.
Christina of Sweden

The queen did fish for men's souls, and had so sweet a bait that no one could escape her network.
Christopher Hatton *(1540-91), English courtier, of Elizabeth I*

She's more of a man than I expected.
Henry James *(1843-1916), US novelist, of Queen Victoria,* Diary *of E.M. Forster*

We few, we happy few, we band of brothers;
For he today that sheds his blood with me
Shall be my brother; be he ne'er so vile
This day shall gentle his condition;
And gentlemen in England now a-bed
Shall think themselves accursed they were not here,
And hold their manhoods cheap whiles any speaks
That fought with us upon Saint Crispin's day.
King Henry in Henry V *by* **William Shakespeare**

A great man does enough for us when he refrains
from doing us harm.
Pierre de Beaumarchais (1732-99), *French playwright,*
The Barber of Seville, *1775*

Great men, like great cities, have many crooked arts,
and dark alleys in their hearts, whereby he that
knows them may save himself much time and
trouble.
Charles Caleb Colton (c. 1780-1832), *clergyman,*
sportsman and gambler, Lacon, *1825*

Men of less principle and honesty than I pretend to
look on public measures and opinions as a game; I
always act from conviction.
George III

As far as mortal man can guide the course of things
when he is gone, the course of our national history
since William's day has been the result of William's
character and of William's acts. Well may we
restore to him the surname that men gave him in
his own day. He may worthily take his place as
William the Great alongside Alexander,
Constantine, and Charles.
E.A. Freeman, *(1823-92), English historian,* William the
Conqueror

William, indeed, seems to have been astute without
wisdom, resolute without foresight, powerful
without ultimate purpose, a man of very limited
aims and very limited vision, narrow, ignorant and
superstitious.
R.G. Richardson *and* **G.O. Sayles**, *of William the
Conqueror,* The Governance of Medieval England

Henry I was not a creator of institutions; he contributed nothing to the theory of kingship or to the philosophy of government. He created men. It was his contribution to English government and society to insert into the social fabric men with a direct interest in royal government; men who depended on royal government for their rise, and on its continuance for their survival.

R.W. Southern, The Place of Henry I in English History

MEN AND WOMEN

Fool! Don't you see now that I could have poisoned you a hundred times had I been able to live without you!

Cleopatra, to Mark Antony

She was the greatest of Englishwomen – I had almost said of Englishmen – for she added the highest manly qualities of the personal delicacy of the woman.

Joseph Chamberlain (1836-1914), British statesman, of *Queen Victoria, in a letter to Lord Milner, 25 January 1901*

Lady Elizabeth was very unlike the cocktail-drinking, chain-smoking girls who came to be regarded as typical of the nineteen-twenties. The radiant vitality, and a blending of gaiety, kindness and sincerity, made her irresistible to men.

Lady Airlie, describing Elizabeth Bowes-Lyon (now Queen Mother)

They [Englishmen] find it impossible to know how to deal with hysterical women. If one has a row with them, they invariably leave the room or disappear.

Barbara Cartland, on why the Prince of Wales could not resolve differences with Princess Diana

MISTRESSES

O Sire, it were better to be your mistress than your wife.
Catherine Parr, *sixth wife of Henry VIII, in reply to his proposal of marriage*

She is the only woman in France who makes me forget I am a sexagenarian.
Louis XV, *King of France (1710-74), speaking of his mistress, Madame du Barry, Countess L'Esparbes*

'You have slept with every one of my subjects!'
She answered bashfully, 'Oh Sire'
'You have had the Duc de Choiseul'
'He is so powerful'
'The Marechal de Richelieu'
'He is so witty'
'Monville'
'He has such beautiful legs'
'Very well. But what about the Duc d'Aumont, who has nothing of all this?'
'Ah, Sire, he – he is so devoted to your majesty!'
That shouldn't hamper your marrying.
Queen Caroline, *(1638-1737), in reply to her husband, George II, when on her deathbed she urged him to marry again. He replied had that he would have mistresses*

Hard by the Mall lives a wench called Nell,
King Charles the Second he kept her
She hath got a trick to handle his pr---,
But never lays hands on his sceptre.
All matters of state from her soul she does haste,
And leave to the politic bitches.
The whore's in the right, for 'tis her delight
To be scratching just where it itches.
Anon., *of Nell Gwyn, 1650-87*

His recommending only his mistresses and their children to his brother's care would have been a strange conclusion to any other's life, but was well enough suited to all the other parts of his.
Gilbert Burnet, *of Charles II*, History of My Own Time

Permit me, Sir, to help you to a whore:
Kiss her but once, you'll ne'r want Cleveland more.
She's Buckhurst's whore at present, but you know –
When sovereign wants a whore, the subject must
forgo.
Sir George Etherege (c. 1635-92), *Restoration dramatist,
dedicated to Charles II about Nell Gwyn*

Let not poor Nelly starve.
Charles II, *when dying, referring to Nell Gwyn*

A royal mistress should curtsey first then jump into
bed.
Alice Keppel, *mistress of Edward VII*

My great-grandmother was your great-great-
grandfather's mistress. How about it?
Camilla Parker-Bowles, *to Prince Charles at their first
meeting in the 1960s. (Her great grandmother was Alice
Keppel)*

When you saw them together, even if you didn't
know the past, you could tell that there had been
something going on.
Princess Diana, *referring to Prince Charles and Camilla
Parker-Bowles*, Daily Mail, *May 1993*

It is perhaps no coincidence that his father seemed
to single out wealthy, influential and sometimes
married women for conquests, me included. I think
John has the same approach. I think he is head over
heels for her, but I have to say, with regret, that the
fact she is married to the Queen's son and has access
to future millions will have helped.
Pamela Bryan, *former step-mother of John Bryan,
speaking on an American television programme of her son's
relationship with the Duchess of York*

I haven't seen the woman for 15 years. I don't
know her. I don't know where she lives. I don't have
any contact with her and I don't know why she is
saying this. I'm glad [heavy sarcasm] she's acting as
my PR woman, but I wish she'd stop.
John Bryan, *speaking after his former step-mother's
television interview, the* Sun, *August 1992*

MODESTY

His way of arguing was very civil and patient, for he seldom contradicted another by his authority, but by his reason; nor did he by any petulant dislike quash another's arguments.
Sir Philip Warwick, *of King Charles I*

MONARCHY

The monarchy is the oldest profession in the world.
Prince Charles

All the time I feel I must justify my existence.
Prince Charles

You should settle in France, Sir. And it would make Royalty popular here.
Judic, *French actress, to Albert Edward, Prince of Wales*

. . . Thank you, but you use up your Kings at too fast a rate in this country.
Prince Albert Edward's riposte

Every day seems to bring us closer to the collapse of the monarchy.
Michael Aspel, *radio/TV personality, 1992*

Diana is the acceptable face of the British monarchy – if they lose her services it is a great blow.
Robert Kilroy-Silk, *TV host, 1992*

Altogether the cost of the state of the monarchy is probably not less than two million pounds a year – as much as Omo and Daz spend on advertising.
Anthony Sampson, *British journalist, author, 1965*

I was taught a kind of theoretic republicanism which was prepared to tolerate a monarch so long as he recognised that he was an employee of the people and subject to dismissal if he proved unsatisfactory.

My grandfather, who was no respecter of persons, used to explain this point of view to Queen Victoria and she was not altogether sympathetic.
Betrand Russell *(1872-1970), English philosopher and mathematician,* Portraits from memory, *1956*

. . . The prestige of the monarchy, and the influence of the monarchy, in the prudent and conscientious hands of King George have waxed rather than waned . . . No cabinet, however strong, could afford to disregard the difficulties and doubts put forward by a sovereign who has no interest in party politics, and whose experience is reinforced by continuity and immutability.
Earl of Birkenhead *(1872-1930), of George V,* America Revisited

He was the first English king who was a good European. The least forthcoming and the most inscrutable of monarchs, he nevertheless familiarised men with a new type of kingship, detached, dignified, and, in all impersonal matters, essentially just.
David Ogg, *of William IV,* England in the Reigns of James II and William III

A monarch frequently represents his subjects better than an elected assembly; and if he is a good judge of character he is likely to have more capable and loyal advisors.
William Ralph Inge *(1860-1954), English divine, 'Our Present Discontents',* Outspoken Essays, First Series, *1919*

Monarchs are always surrounded with refined spirits, so penetrating that they frequently discover in their masters great qualities, invisible to vulgar eyes, and which, did they not publish them to mankind, would be unobserved for ever.
Dr Johnson, Marmor Norfolciense, *1739*

Love between monarchs never reaches the nuptial stage, for reasons of state – far stronger than these knots – have no trouble in finding the means of extinguishing these ardours.
Pierre Corneille

In the whole Kingdom there is only one man who makes the moves, that's the monarch; all the rest just stand to attention.
Denis Diderot

King Charles the First, after he was condemned, did tell Colonel Tomlinson, that he believed, That the English Monarchy was now at an end; About half an hour later, he told the Colonel, That now he had assurance by a strong impulse on his spirit, that his son should reign after him. This information I had from Fabian Phillips Esq of the Inner-Temple, who had good authority for the truth of it.
John Aubrey

Wilson comes closest to understanding the peculiar attractions of the monarchy to the English. The Scots and the Australians may not care for it but it appeals to the dreaminess and romanticism of the English, as well as a bloody minded determination not to be quite like the rest of Europe.
John Mortimer, on A.N. Wilson's The Rise and Fall of the House of Windsor

No one in Europe seriously wants a monarchy. People are in favour of democracy.
German MP, 1992

. . . Why should a Hun want to dismantle a Hanovarian monarchy?
Sir Nicholas Fairbairn, Tory MP, in riposte

As we move ever more closely into the heart of the European Community, the relevance of the monarchy will grow greater, not less. What people fear we will lose in the abstractions of Brussels is our sense of nationhood: thanks to the monarchy, around which all those feelings of historic pride constellate, we shall not do so.
Lord St John of Fawsley, *in an article in support of the monarchy*, Daily Mail

He saw then the extent to which the whole Empire might stand or fall by the personal example set from the throne, and to insure the integrity of that example he was to sacrifice much that men hold dear, much that makes life sweet.
Biographer of George V, of the overwhelming manifestations of loyalty that George V met while on his world tours

The institution of monarchy to which, rightly or wrongly I belong and which I represent to the best of my ability, is one of the strongest factors in the continuance of a stable government.
Prince Charles, *addressing a joint session of the New South Wales Parliament in Sydney, 1974*

From this time forward, under God [the reference to God is optional] I pledge my loyalty to Australia and its people, whose democratic beliefs I share, whose rights and liberties I respect, and whose laws I will uphold and obey.
Paul Keating, *Australian Prime Minister, proposing a new oath of allegiance to go before the Australian parliament, expunging references to the Queen*

Most Australians, even many royalists, now expect that they will never see a King Charles III as their head of state. For a majority, though many of them are sad about it, the monarchy is a dead letter.
Mike Carlton, *presenter on LBC Newstalk radio, in the* Sunday Times, *December 1992*

Like the hansom cab, the monarchy has a certain elegance. But it is of little use in this century.
Anon.

MONEY

Fortune hath somewhat the nature of a woman; if she be too much wooed, she is farther off.
Charles V, *Holy Roman Emperor, Francis Bacon*, The Advancement of Learning, *1605*

In private life he would have been called an honest blockhead; and fortune, that made him a king, added nothing to his happiness, only prejudiced his honesty, and shortened his days. No man was ever more free from ambition; he loved money, but loved to keep his own, without being rapacious of other men's!
Lady Mary Wortley Montague *(1689-1762), English writer, of George I, Lewis Melville*, The First George

Early one morning he met a boy in the stables at Windsor and said, 'Well, boy! what do you do? 'What do they pay you?' 'I help in the stable,' said the boy, 'But they only give me victuals and clothes.' 'Be content,' said George, 'I have no more.'
Beckles Wilson, *George III*

I've heard these rumours that my mother has £6.5 billion. Absolute crap! If only she had £6.5 billion!
Prince Edward

Do you know any history authors who make money? What a wonderful, encouraging thought that would be, but I'll have to speed up on one book every five years if I want to make a profit.
Princess Michael of Kent, *when asked if she wrote for money, 1992*

MORALITY

I will rather risk my crown than do what I think personally disgraceful, and whilst I have no wish but for the good and prosperity of my country, it is impossible that the nation shall not stand by me, if they will not, they shall have another King.
George III, *to Lord North, March 1778*

He would fain and despot, even at the cost of being another's Underling . . . I look at him as one of the Monsters of History.
Samuel Taylor Coleridge, *of Charles II, annotation to Lord Braybrooke's Edition of Samuel Pepys's* Diary

MOTHERHOOD

A mother, if physically capable, whether regal or otherwise, ought to supply nature's food to her own offspring.
Letter to the Lancet, *referring to Queen Victoria's refusal to breastfeed her children, 1840*

The Duchess, especially with the children, can't go out and do a job.
Margaret Bennett, *divorce lawyer acting for the Duchess of York, 1992*

Fergie is to motherhood what her husband Andrew is to nuclear physics.
Vernon Coleman, *The* Sun

With animals you don't see the male caring for the offspring. It's against nature. It is a woman's prerogative and duty, and a privilege.
Princess Grace of Monaco

I am very fortunate I have a darling husband and two wonderful children, and we're all healthy.

That's what matters.
Princess Michael of Kent, *1992*

MOTTO

Dieu et mon droit. [God and my right.]
Richard I, *originally used as a war cry, September 1198, now the motto on the royal arms of Great Britain*

En toute chose on doit tenir le moyen. [Always keep a balanced view of everything]
Anne de Beaujeau, *Duchess de Bourbon, daughter of Louis XI, final instruction in a* Guide to Education, *expounding the highest ideals and moral principles*

Omnium victorem vici. [I conquered him who conquers all]
Sole vivit in illo. [She only lives through him]
Diane de Poitiers

Courage – and shuffle the cards.
*Motto of **Lola Montez** (1818-61), mistress of King Ludwig I of Bavaria*

Ich dien. [I serve.]
Traditional motto of the Prince of Wales

MUSIC

I know the song ('There was an old man who had a sow') and I can make all those noises at home but I cannot do them with my tiara on.
The Queen

Oh, do turn it off, it is so embarrassing unless one is there – like hearing the Lord's Prayer when playing canasta.
Queen Elizabeth the Queen Mother, *on hearing the national anthem played at a televised cup final*

For instrumental music there is a certain Haydn, who has some peculiar ideas, but he is only just beginning.
Maria Theresa, *Holy Roman Empress in a letter to Archduchess Marie Beatrix, 1772*

You ask my opinion about taking the young Salzburg musician Mozart into your service. I do not know where you can place him, since I feel that you do not require a composer or any other useless people . . . it gives one's service a bad name, when such types go about the world like beggars; besides, he has a large family.
Maria Theresa, *in a letter to her son, Emperor Joseph II*

NEGOTIATIONS

Up to 24 hours before the official separation
announcement was made, there was some hard
bargaining going on at the Palace.
*A royal aide, referring to the separation of the Prince and
Princess of Wales*

The Queen and Philip were trying to find a solution
to the crisis and called in the Prime Minister and the
Foreign Office. The FO had already drawn up a
short list of five possible countries and Charles was
definitely sold. He was prepared to 'take a holiday'
with the honour of Governor. He said he would
take two years out in a bid to patch up the marriage.
But Diana would have none of it.
*A royal aide referring to the separation of the Prince and
Princess of Wales*

NICKNAMES

Old Rowley.
*In some of the State poems, Charles II is ridiculed under
the nick-name of Old Rowley, which was an ill-favoured
stallion. It was remarkable for getting fine colts. – Mrs
Holford, a young lady much admired by Charles, was
sitting in her apartment and singing a satirical ballad
upon 'Old Rowley the King', when he knocked at the
door. Upon her asking who was there? he, with his usual
good humour replied, 'Old Rowley himself, Madam'*

Bluff King Hal.
King Henry VIII

Good Queen Bess.
Queen Elizabeth I

No one ever gave Henry the VII a nickname. He never seems to have caught the popular imagination. What contemporaries chiefly remarked in him was his wisdom, by which they meant his sound common sense. Men feared him, admired him, depended on him, but they did not love him.
Conyers Read (1881-1959), *US author*, The Tudors

The rottweiller.
The name **Princess Diana** *has given to Camilla Parker-Bowles*

The Wicked stepmother, and Acid Raine.
Name given to Raine, second wife of Earl Spencer and step-mother to Princess Diana

Fergie.
The Duchess of York

The Duke of Pork.
The Duke of York (used in Canada)

Ned of Wales.
Harry Secombe, ex-Goon and friend of Prince Charles

Foggy.
Captain Mark Philips, ex-husband of Princess Anne

Princess Pushy.
Princess Michael of Kent

Squidgy.
Name said to have been used for Princess Diana by her close friend James Gilbey on what became known as the Squidgy tapes

Gladys.
*Name used for Camilla Parker-Bowles by Prince Charles on
the alleged Camillagate tapes*

NOBILITY

The nobility of England, my lord, would have
snored through the Sermon on the Mount.
Sir Thomas More to Henry VIII, in A Man for All Seasons,
by **Robert Bolt**

NUDITY

I have seen three emperors in their nakedness and
the sight was not inspiring.
Prince Otto von Bismark

Naked came I out of my mother's womb and naked
shall I return thither.
*Priest quoting from Job on King Frederick the Great's
deathbed*
No. Not quite naked. I shall have a uniform on.
King Frederick's *reply*

In our way discoursing of the wantonness of the
Court and how it minds nothing else. And I saying
that that would leave the King shortly, if he did not
leave it, he told me 'No', for the King doth spend
most of his time in feeling and kissing them naked
all over their bodies in bed – and contents himself,
without doing all the other but as he finds himself
inclined; but this lechery will never leave him.
Samuel Pepys, *of Charles II*, Diary, *16 October 1655*

OBEDIENCE

A man born to obey will obey even on a throne.
Luc de Clapiers, Marquis de Vauvenargues (1715-
47), *French moralist and soldier* Reflections and Maxims,
1746

OPTIMISM

Now we can look the East End in the face.
Elizabeth the Queen Mother, *then the wife of King
George VI, surveying the damage caused to Buckingham
Palace by a bomb during the Blitz in World War II*

Thank God, I am an optimist, and I believe in the
common sense of the people of this country.
George V *in a letter to a friend*

There's no point worrying about what might have
been. Whatever the position there are advantages
and disadvantages, and one balances out the other.
I'm delighted to be where I am for a variety of
reasons. At the same time I regret it for a great many
other reasons.
Prince Philip, *on his 65th birthday, referring to his role as
consort to Queen Elizabeth II*

PAIN

This you'd believe, had I but the time to tell you,
The pain it costs to poor laborious Nelly
While she employs hands, fingers, lips and thighs
E'ere she can raise the Member she enjoys.
John Wilmot, *Earl of Rochester of Nell Gwyn*

PALLAS

Although it's a pretty naughty affair I think
members of the Royal Family will be amused despite
the reality of the situation. After the first series I
heard from somebody who was at Sandringham last
Christmas and they said the young Royals really
enjoyed it.
Kate Robbins, *actress, speaking of the TV series* Pallas.
*Kate Robbins supplies the voice-overs for the Queen,
Duchess of York and Princess Anne in the series*

PASSION

For something like five years she succeeded in holding him at arms' length, a remarkable performance, all things considered, and probably indicative that there was considerably more of cold calculation than of passion in Anne's attitude.
Conyers Read, *of Anne Boleyn,* The Tudors

Save your energy for later darling, you'll need it.
The Duchess of York, *to Prince Andrew, while on a skiing holiday in Klosters, February 1987*

Close to, the man struck terror in my heart. What an extraordinary man! He was like a volcano. The passion which dominated him was not love – which, though violent, was transitory – but ambition.
Marie Walewska (1786-1817), *mistress of Napoleon I*

Charles cannot live without her.
Annabel Elliot, *sister of Camilla Parker-Bowles*

PATIENCE

He gets irritated with her [the Queen's] passiveness. You see, she's much better at knowing when it's right to say no, than at taking the initiative and saying yes. So he'll say, 'Come on, Lillibet. Come on, just do it!' She in turn gets cross with his bad temper. Once, when he threatened to walk out of a lengthy sitting for a portrait, she coolly ordered, 'You stand there!'.
Royal courtier, of Queen Elizabeth and Prince Philip, quoted in the Independent on Sunday, *December 1992*

Be patient. Because of you, your country is very dear to me now.
Emperor Napoleon I *of France, to Marie Walewska, his Polish mistress*

PATRONAGE

Every time I bestow a vacant office I make a hundred discontented persons and one ingrate.
Louis XIV

PEACE

Peace is necessary to the vast empire. We need population not devastation.
Catherine the Great

Try to keep peace with your neighbours. I have loved war too much; do not copy me in that nor in my extravagance.
Louis XIV, *remark to his great-grandson, the future Louis XV*

I have many times asked myself whether there can be more potent advocates of peace upon earth through the years to come than this massed multitude of silent witnesses to the desolation of war.
George V, *referring to the massed World War graves in Flanders, 1922,* Silent Cities, *ed. Gavin Stamp*

Remember! . . . I go from a Corruptible to an Incorruptible crown where no disturbances can be, but Peace and Joy for evermore.
Charles II, *when called to the scaffold for high treason*

As I have counselled you to be slow in taking on a war, so advise I you to be slow in peace-making. Before ye agree look that the ground of your wars to be satisfied in your peace, and that ye see a good a good surety for you and your people: otherways, an honourable and just war is more tolerable than a dishonourable and disadvantageous peace.
James I and VI

PERFECTION

There were some moral and social values in his perfection in little things. He could not keep the Ten Commandments, but he kept the ten thousand commandments. His name is unconnected with any great acts of duty or sacrifice, but it is connected with a great many of those acts of magnanimous politeness, of a kind of dramatic delicacy which lie on the dim borderland between morality and art.
G.K. Chesterton *(1874-1936), English critic, novelist and poet, of Charles II*

PHOTOGRAPHERS

If photographers want to behave like that, it's their job. I guess. Next time I will just have 15 rottweilers wherever I go – growly ones. Or I shall go around with a spade and dig the ground up just to make sure no one is underneath it.
The Duchess of York

Let's go to the future and perhaps hope that photographers don't build trenches in woods, on private land, two-and-a-half miles from the road and crawl on their tummies like snakes to get those photographs of a very happy scene with very, very happy children.
The Duchess of York, *on holiday with her children, when asked about the topless pictures in the press of her and John Bryan, 1992*

Haven't you run out of film yet?
Prince Charles *to photographers*

Get these bloody cameras away from the Queen.
Prince Philip, *to photographers on a walkabout*

You bloody load of clots! You could take pictures like this any Sunday at home in Windsor, yet you come all the way to Jamaica to do it.
Prince Philip, *to photographers, on a visit to Jamaica, 1963*

PITY

Princess Margaret: Does that mean you will be the next queen?
Princess Elizabeth: Yes, some day.
Princess Margaret: Poor you.

PLAY

If all the year were playing holidays,
To sport would be as tedious as to work.
Prince Hal in King Henry IV part 1 *by* **William Shakespeare**

PLEASURE

He [Charles II] said once to myself, he was no atheist, but he could not think God would make a man miserable only for taking a little pleasure out of the way.
Gilbert Burnet, History of My Own Time

The dandy of sixty, who bows with a grace,
And has taste in wigs, collars, cuirasses, and lace;
Who to tricksters and fools leaves the State and its
treasure,
And, while Britain's in tears, sails about at his
pleasure.
William Hone (1780-1842), *English writer and*
bookseller, of George IV, The Political House that Jack Built

POLITENESS

Punctuality is the politeness of the kings.
Louis XVIII (1755-1824), *King of France, attrib.*

POLITICS

Today 23 years ago dear Grandmama died. I
wonder what she would have thought of a Labour
government
George V, *on the formation of the first Labour government*

Well, what are you socialists going to do about me?
George V, *to Ramsay MacDonald at his first meeting as*
Prime Minister

A form of government that is not the result of a long
sequence of shared experiences, efforts, and
endeavours can never take root.
Napoleon I, *J. Christopher Herlod,* The Mind of
Napoleon, *1955*

Royal clemency is often but a political manoeuvre to
gain the nation's affection.
François, Duc de La Rochefoucald

Lord John Russell may resign, and Lord Aberdeen
may resign, but I can't resign.
Queen Victoria, *speaking to Lord Clarendon on the*
formation of a government, January 1855

Ye politicians, tell me, pray,
      Why thus with woe and care rent?
This is the worst you can say, –
Some wind has blown the Whig away,
      And left the Heir Apparent.
Charles Lamb (1775-1834), *English essayist, of George IV*

Of political dexterity and artifice he was altogether
incapable, and although if he had been false, able,
and artful, he might have caused more perplexity to
his Whig government and have played a better party
game, it is perhaps fortunate for the country and
certainly happy for his own reputation, that his
virtues thus predominated over his talents.
Charles Greville, *of William IV*, Diary, *25 June 1837*

My new government is not too easy and the people
are rather difficult to talk to.
George VI, *speaking of the Labour government, 1945*

POPULATION

Polygamy is useful for the purpose of population.
Catherine the Great

POTENTIAL

These are rare attainments for a damsel, but pray
tell me, can she spin?
James I, *on being introduced to a young girl proficient in
Latin, Greek and Hebrew*

POVERTY

I want there to be no peasant in my realm so poor
that he will not have a chicken in his pot every
Sunday.
Henri IV, *(Henri of Navarre) (1553-1610), attrib.*

POWER

Be the Emperor, be Peter the Great, John the
terrible, The Emperor Paul – crush them all under
you – now don't you laugh naughty one – but I long
to see you so with those men who try to govern you
and it must be the contrary.
Alexandra, *Empress Consort of Russia, letter to Nicholas
II, 1916*

Power without a nation's confidence is nothing.
Catherine the Great

You will have heard of our taking of New
Amsterdam . . . It did belong to England heretofore,
but the Dutch by degrees drove our people out and
built a very good town, but we have got the better of
it, and 'tis now called New York.
Charles II, *October 1664*

The power of kings is founded on the reason and on
the folly of the people, and specially on their folly.
Blaise Pascal *(1623-62), French mathematician and
philosopher, Pensées, 1669*

He who has the greatest power put into his hands
will only become more impatient of any restraints in
the use of it.
William Hazlitt, On the Spirit of the Monarchy, *1823*

She was with regard to power as some men are to
their amours, the vanity of being thought to possess
what she desired was equal to the pleasure of the
possession itself.
Lord Hervey, *of Caroline Wilhelmina of Ansbach, Queen
Consort to George II, Memoirs*

If he is to be blamed, it must not be for what he did,
but for what he was – an unbalanced man of low
intelligence. And if he is to be praised, it is because
he attempted to discharge honourably tasks that
were beyond his powers.
J.H. Plumb, *of George III*

Murmurings of children in a dream. The royal project of gracious interposition with our rivals is a mere phantom. It pleases the vanity of a court deprived of substantial power . . .
Benjamin Disraeli, *letter to Lord Derby concerning Queen Victoria's offer to mediate with the Liberals, 21 October 1866*

She's tasted power and she assumes she can wield it as never before.

She wasn't prepared to tolerate a shared life with a man she detests. But neither did she want to discard the trappings and the magic. At the moment she seems to be victorious. She may have bitter regrets when she finds the court she has created is treated more as show business than regal.
The Daily Mail, *of Princess Diana, December 1992*

The foremost art of kings is the power to endure hatred.
Seneca *(c.4 BC–c.AD65), Roman philosopher, statesman and tragedian,* Hercules Furens

PRAISE

The king praises no one whom he has not resolved to ruin.
Bishop Bloet, *of Henry I,* History of England, *translated by T. Forester*

The King daylie and nightlie in his owne person visited and searched the watches, orders and stacions of euerie part of his hoast, and whom he founde dilligent he praised and thanked, and the negligent he corrected and chastised.
Anon., *of Henry V's conduct during a seige,* The First English Life of King Henry the Fifth

PREGNANCY

I've become much more mature and responsible. I feel womanly. It's an intense pleasure.
Princess Stephanie *of Monaco, on her pregnancy, 1992*

PRESERVATION

Do we really need to compress the traditions and
vitality of rural life and culture into the straitjacket
of an industry like any other?
Prince Charles, *in a speech in praise of France's attempts
to preserve uneconomic rural ways of life, Paris, 1992*

The Prince should be defending the people of this
country who have to pay £16 a week per family
extra to support French farmers and their food.
Dr Robert Spink, *Tory MP, commenting on Prince
Charles's support of the French farmers*

The Prince seems particularly attached to the rural
idyll, into which harsh reality seems to him to be an
inconvenience.
Andrew Hargreaves, *Tory MP*

PRESS

I thought you must have been lying on the ground
looking up my skirt.
Princess Diana, *to members of the press*

The freedom of the press works in such a way that
there is not much freedom from it.
Princess Grace of Monaco

You won't need me now you've got Fergie.
Princess Diana, *to photographers*

You cannot take quotations in newspapers
seriously. It so happens that it is perfectly legal to
put anything in quotation marks, and there is
nothing you can do about it. You have no copyright
on what other people say you said. There's no point
in talking about it!
Prince Philip, *the* Independent on Sunday, *December 1992*

Lady D: Is there anything in the newspapers this morning Withers?
Withers: They have named another battleship after Queen Victoria, madam.
Lady D: Another! She must be beginning to think there is some resemblance.
Alan Bennett, Forty Years On, 1968

Last week lawyers acting for the Duchess of York initiated discussions about a formal separation for the Duke and Duchess. These discussions are not yet complete and nothing more will be said until they are.

The Queen hopes that the media will spare the Duke and Duchess of York and their children any intrusion.
Official statement issued by Buckingham Palace, 1992

Do we really want to continue down the road to a hideous world where, not just the royal family but anyone who gets into the goldfish bowl of public life, can have their slightest move from the conventional path intruded on and then paraded as if on a gallows before its slavering public.
Michael Shea, *the Queen's former press secretary*

No blondes with me today.
Prince Charles, *to waiting photographers as he stepped off a train in Scotland, 1992*

I don't know what he would have said if I had turned him down.
Earl Spencer, *father of Lady Diana Spencer, to reporters, referring to Prince Charles's request for his permission to marry his daughter*

May I ask the editors of Fleet Street whether, in the execution of their jobs, they consider it necessary or fair to harass my daughter daily from dawn until well after dusk.
The Hon. Mrs Shand-Kydd, *mother of Diana Spencer, in a letter to* The Times, *1980*

Regrettably, it does not make news to know that fifty jumbo jets landed safely at London airport yesterday, but it does make news if one doesn't. I still believe, however, in the necessity every now and then of reminding people, metaphorically, that vast numbers of jumbos do land safely – for the simple reason that we are all human, and the maintenance of our morale needs careful consideration.
Prince Charles, *presenting the British Press Awards and addressing assembled editors and proprietors of Fleet Street, 1978*

Yes, there may be a gutter press and yes, it does sometimes offend not only those of a finer sensibility but us all. But it may be that journalists belong in the gutter because it is in the gutter that the secrets of the ruling class are to be found.
London Evening Standard, *January 1993*

With great admiration and respect to you and your job, and with my very best manners, I would like to decline your generous and kind offer.
John Bryan *to a reporter, declining to discuss his relationship with the Duchess of York*

PRESSURE

You could feel it underneath . . . I don't know how long he can last . . . bottled up like that.
Ex-King **Peter of Yugoslavia** *to his wife after lunching at Buckingham Palace at the time of George VI's death, referring to Prince Philip, Duke of Edinburgh*

My God! That guy works so hard you'd think he was running for office.
Remark by an awe-struck American journalist during Prince Charles's American tour, 1977

PRIDE

Pride has a greater share than goodness of heart in the remonstrances we make to those who are guilty of faults; we reprove not so much with a view to correct them as to persuade them that we are exempt from those faults ourselves.
François, Duc de La Rochefoucauld

Move Queen Anne? Most certainly not! Why it might some day be suggested that my statue should be moved, which I should much dislike.
Queen Victoria, *at the time of her Diamond Jubilee, 1897, when it was suggested that the statue of Queen Anne should be moved from outside St Paul's*

PRINCES

Princes are like heavenly bodies, which cause good and evil times, and which have much veneration, but no rest.
Francis Bacon, 'Of Empire', Essays, 1625

Where princes are concerned, a man who is able to do good is as dangerous and almost as criminal as a man who intends to do evil.
Cardinal De Retz (1614-79), Memoirs, 1655

A prince is a gr'reat man in th' ol' counthry, but he niver is as gr'reat over there as he is here [in America]
Finley Peter Dunne, *'Prince Henry's Reception'*, Observations by Mr Dooley, 1902

A prince should always be a perfect model of virtue, all the more since he lives in a glass house. If, however, we yield in spite of ourselves, we must observe two precautions . . . First, that the time allotted to a liaison should never prejudice our affairs . . . Secondly – and more difficult to practise – that in giving our heart we must maintain absolute master of our mind.
Louis XIV, Testament Politique

When a prince giveth any man a very extravagant reward it looketh as if it was rather for an ill thing than a good one.
Marquess of Halifax, Political Thoughts and Reflections, *late seventeenth century*

Princes have this remaining of humanity, that they think themselves obliged not to make war without a reason.
Dr Johnson, 'Memoirs of the King of Prussia', 1756

To enjoy a prince's favour does not rule out the possibility of merit, but neither does it argue for its existence.
Jean de la Bruyere, 'Of Opinions', Caractères, 1688

How necessary it is for a prince to get his basic principles right; otherwise he is certain to be ruined.
Niccolò Machiavelli, The Prince

There is no set-out role for me. It depends entirely what I make of it . . . I'm really rather an awkward problem.
Prince Charles, *speaking of his future role*

He's a prince isn't he? So let him get on with being a prince.
Senator Agnelli, *on being asked to find a job at Fiat for an Austrian prince, who married into his family*

He was a prince, sad, serious and full of thoughts, and secret observations, and full of notes and memorials of his own hand, especially touching persons. As, who to employ, whom to reward, whom to inquire of, whom to beware of, what were the dependencies, what were the factions, and the like; keeping, as it were, a journal of his thoughts.
Francis Bacon, History of the Reign of Henry VII

It never did me any good to be a Prince, I can tell
you, and many was the time I wished I hadn't been.
It was a pretty tough place and, so far from making
any allowances for our disadvantages, the other
boys made a point of taking it out on us on the
grounds that they'd never be able to do it later on
. . . they used to make me go up and challenge the
bigger boys – I was awfully small then – and I'd get
a hiding time and again.
George V, *explaining that there was no featherbedding in
the Navy for Princes*, *Sir John Wheeler-Bennett*, King George
VI: His Life and Reign, *1965*

Not a fatter fish than he
Flounders round the polar sea.
See his blubbers – at his gills
What a world of drink he swills . . .
Every fish of generous kind
Scuds aside or shrinks behind;
But about his presence keep
All the monsters of the deep . . .
Name or title what has he? . . .
Is he Regent of the sea?
By his bulk and by his size,
By his oily qualities,
This (or else my eyesight fails),
This should be the Prince of Whales.
Anon., The Prince of Whales, c. *late nineteenth century*

PRIVILEGE

There are privileges. It's swings and roundabouts.
We live in this lovely house, rent free, which is so
quiet you can hear owls at night. I can usually get to
Wimbledon and tickets to a popular show or
aeroplane seats when bookings are very full.

   Also, it may not make sense, but one is in a
position to do a certain amount of good – make
causes more known.
Princess Michael of Kent, *in an interview for* Good
Housekeeping, *on being asked if it was a drag being a royal*

PROFESSIONAL

Everything he turns his hand to is approached the
same way. He is totally professional. He takes care
to brief himself extremely well. And he really knows
his stuff. No one else does a job quite as well as he.
Lord Buxton, *of Prince Philip. Lord Buxton works with
the Prince at the World Wide Fund for Nature*

PROMISCUITY

She is like measles. Everybody should go through
the experience. Once you've had it, you never want
to have it again.
*A victim of the Grand Duchess Anastasia, notorious during
the 1930s for entertaining young men*

In the Isle of Great Britain long since famous
known,
For breeding the best C—— in Christendom;
There reigns, and long may he reign and thrive,
The easiest Prince and best bred man alive:
Him no ambition moves to seek Renown,
Like the French fool to wander up and down,
Starving his subjects, hazarding his Crown.
Nor are his high desires above his strength:
His scepter and his P—— are of a length,
And she that plays with one may sway the other,
And make him little wiser than his brother . . .
Poor Prince, the P—— like the Buffoons at Court,
It governs thee because it makes thee sport;
Tho' Safety, Law, Religion, Life, lay on't,
'Twill break through all to its way to C——,
Restless he rolls about from Whore to Whore
A merry Monarch, scandalous and poor.
John Wilmot, *Earl of Rochester, of Charles II. As a result
of the poem, Wilmot was banished from court*

PROMISES

Whatever he may promise, he will break everything
to get a regular income from his parliament.
Louis XIV, *referring to Charles II of England in a letter to*
Barildon, 1680

. . . A wise, discreet, honest and sincere courtier,
who will promise no farther than she can perform,
and will always perform what she does promise.
Lady Betty Germaine, *referring to Henrietta Howard,*
Countess of Suffolk and mistress of George II, in a letter to
Jonathan Swift, 8 February 1733

PROPAGANDA

If *we* do not then remember that a licensed press is
the press of the Establishment. It will only print that
news that the governing classes wish the people to
know. A free press is a press of the people. It tells the
people what the governing classes wish to conceal
from them. As Lord Northcliffe once memorably
put it: news is what someone somewhere doesn't
want you to know. All else is propaganda.
The London Evening Standard, *defending freedom of*
the press in response to accusations that the British press has
damaged the reputation of the Royal family, January 1993

PROVERBS AND SAYINGS

Noblesse oblige.
A French phrase meaning noble birth imposes the
obligation of noble action

Queen Anne is dead.
A sarcastic way of saying 'That's old news'

There is no royal road to learning.
*The royal road to anything is a way of attaining it without
effort, since the king's way (the royal road) is always made
easy for him. One cannot attain learning – that is, knowledge
got by study – without hard work*

Rivers and kings are not to be trusted.
Arab proverb

Only with a new ruler do you realise the value of the
old.
Burmese proverb

He who would rule must hear and be deaf, see and
be blind.
German proverb

PUSHY

Pushy? Just ambitious.
Princess Michael of Kent, *in an interview when asked if
she minded being labelled Princess Pushy by the press,
September 1992*

QUEEN

You have chosen me from a low estate to be your
queen and companion, far beyond my desert or
desire.
Anne Boleyn, *in her last letter to Henry VIII*

How different how very different, from the home
life of our own dear Queen!
Anon., *comment of a contemporary woman in the
reign of Queen Victoria after a performance of* Antony and
Cleopatra, *in* A Laugh a Day *by Irvin S. Cobb*

. . . They wished to treat me like a girl, but I will
show them that I am Queen of England.
Queen Victoria, *in a letter to Lord Melbourne on the
Bedchamber Question, May 1839*

Her court was pure; her life serene;
God gave her peace; her land reposed;
A thousand claims to reverence closed
In her as Mother, Wife and Queen.
Alfred, Lord Tennyson *(1809-92), English poet, of*
Queen Victoria, To the Queen

REIGN

To know nor faith, nor love, nor law; to be
omnipotent but friendless is to reign.
Percy Bysshe Shelley *(1792-1822), English poet,*
Prometheus Unbound, *1818-19*

How Monarchs die is easily explain'd
And thus it might upon the Tomb be chisell'd
As long as George the Fourth could reign he reign'd
And then he mizzled.
Thomas Hood *(1799-1845), English poet and humourist,*
of George IV, On a Royal Demise

As a son, as a husband, as a father, and especially as
an adviser of young men, I deem it my duty to say
that, on a review of his whole life, I can find no one
good thing to speak of, in either the conduct or the
character of this King; and, as an Englishman, I
should be ashamed to show my head, if I were not to
declare that I deem his reign (including his regency)
to have been the most unhappy for the people that
England has ever known.
William Cobbett *(1763-1835), English writer, of*
George IV, Political Register, *3 July 1830*

REINCARNATION

I'd like to come back in your trousers.
Alleged to have been said by **Prince Charles** *to Camilla*
Parker-Bowles on the Camilla tape

RELATIONSHIPS

Now there's no pressure to make the marriage work, they have become very good, very close friends.
Friend of the Duchess of York speaking to the press about the Duchess's marriage to Prince Andrew

You'd never think Andrew and Fergie were no longer a couple.
A member of staff

How delighted I am with him, and how much I like him in every way. He possesses every quality that could be desired to make me perfectly happy.
Queen Victoria, *of Prince Albert, reporting to her matchmaking uncle, Leopold, King of the Belgians*

I trust they will be very happy. We are delighted, and he looks beaming.
Queen Mary, *referring to the marriage of the future George VI to Elizabeth Bowes-Lyon (now Queen Mother) 1923*

RELIGION

Religion has nothing more to fear than not being sufficiently understood.
Stanislaus, *King of Poland*

A single friar who goes counter to all Christianity for a thousand years must be wrong.
Charles V, *Holy Roman Emperor, referring to Martin Luther*

My father made the most part of you almost out of nothing.
Mary Tudor, *on being threatened during the reign of Edward VI because of her Catholicism*

When the Queen crosses the border she is a Presbyterian.
Radio 4 News, 1992

No bishop, no king.
James II stating that a non-episcopal form of church government was incompatible with the monarchy

Of this you may be assured, that you shall none of you suffer from your opinions or religion, so long as you live peaceably, and you have the word of a king for it.
Charles II, to a deputation of Quakers

Not a religion for gentlemen.
Charles II, referring to Presbyterianism

If in his early travels, and late administration, he seem'd a little biased to one sort of religion; the first is only to be imputed to a certain easiness of temper, and a complaisance for that company he was then forced to keep: and the last was no more than his being tired (which he soon was in any difficulty) with those bold oppositions in Parliament; which made him almost throw himself into the arms of the Roman Catholic party, so remarkable in England for their loyalty, who embrac'd him gladly, and lull'd him asleep with those enchanting songs of absolute sovereignty, which the best and the wisest of Princes are often unable to resist.
John Sheffield, Earl of Mulgrave, A Character of Charles II

It is only too probable that James's bigotry alone baffled his despotism – and that he might have succeeded in suppressing the liberties of his country, if he would – for a time at least – have kept aloof from its Religion. It should be remembered in excuse for the supporters of James II, that, the practicability of conducting the affairs of the state with and by Parliament, had not yet been demonstrated.
Samuel Taylor Coleridge, of James II, annotation to Lord Braybrooke's edition of Pepys's Diary

If he had a point of religion, it was the religion of Mary Tudor's kind, which stirred him to cruelty and revenge and drove him to a career of treason against the religion and freedom of his people.
H.M. Gwatkin, of James II

153

. . . Nothing can be said in his vindication, but that his abolishing Religious Houses and leaving them to the ruinous depredations of time has been of infinite use to the landscape of England in general, which probably was a principal motive for his doing it, since otherwise why should a man who was of no Religion himself be at so much trouble to abolish one which had for ages been established in the Kingdom?
Jane Austen (1775-1817), *English novelist, of Henry VIII*

I die a Christian, according to the profession of the Church of England, as I found it left me by my Father.
Charles I, *on the scaffold, January 1649*

REPUTATION

Most gracious Queen, we implore thee
To go away and sin no more,
But if that effort be too great,
To go away at any rate.
Anon., *referring to Caroline, Queen Consort to George IV, in Lord Colchester, Diary, 15 November 1826*

If I must give up the Princess, I am resolved at least always to think that she would have been respectable if the Prince had behaved only tolerably by her at first.
Jane Austen, *referring to Caroline, Queen consort to George IV, in letter to Matha Lloyd, February 1813*

If she was fit to be introduced as Queen to God she was fit to introduce to men.
Sir Benjamin Bloomfield, *referring to Caroline, Queen consort of George IV in John Wilson Croker, Diary, 6 February 1820*

She [Nell Gwyn] was, or affected to be very orthodox, and a friend to the clergy and the church. The story of her paying the debt of a worthy clergyman, whom, as she was going through the city, she saw some bailiffs hurrying to prison, is a known fact; as is also that of her being insulted in her coach at Oxford by the mob, who mistook her for the Duchess of Portsmouth. Upon which, she looked out of the window, and said, with her usual good humour, 'Pray, good people, be civil; I am the protesant whore!' This laconic speech drew on her the blessings of the populace.

James Granger (1723-76), *English biographer,*
Biographical History of England

King John was not a good man –
He had his little ways,
And sometimes no one spoke to him
For days and days and days.

A.A. Milne (1882-1956), *English author,* Now We Are Six

Unfortunately for his reputation, John was not a great benefactor of monasteries which kept chronicles.

W.C. Warren, King John

John handled the situation [Magna Carta] with a sensitivity to the delicate balance and a resourceful ingenuity which, whatever one thinks of him as a man, can only enhance his reputation as a ruler of consummate ability.

W.C. Warren, King John

Henry VIII perhaps approached as nearly to the ideal standard of perfect wickedness as the infirmities of human nature will allow.

Sir James Mackintosh (1765-1832), History of England
vol. II

Much did she suffer, first on bulk and stage,
From the blackguards and bullies of the age;
Much more her growing virtue did sustain
While dear Charles Hart and Buckhurst su'd in vain.

In vain they su'd; curs'd be the envious tongue
That in her undoubted chastity would wrong;
For should we fame believe, we then might say
That thousands lay with her as well as they.
The Earl of Rochester, *writing about Nell Gwyn and making reference to Hart and Buckhurst, two of Nell's many lovers*

The most impertinent slut in the world.
Mrs Pepys, *wife of Samuel, on hearing the news that Nell Gwyn, Charles II's mistress, was pregnant*

When you met Lola Montez, her reputation made you automatically think of bedrooms.
Aldous Huxley *(1894-1963), English novelist and essayist, of Lola Montez, mistress of King Ludwig I of Bavaria*

The greatest improvement, I fear, will never make him fit for this position.
Queen Victoria, *of her son Edward (later King Edward VII)*

There goes my Uncle Ernest. When I see him I look the other way, there are always some impossible women with him.
Edward VII, *of his uncle Duke Ernest, brother of Prince Albert, explaining to his companion why he jumped into a bush while walking in the Bois de Boulogne*

Whilst Shakespeare gives the worst names to the worst things and makes every improper thing revolting, the French make improper things interesting and gloss wickedness over.
Vicky, Crown Princess of Prussia, *remark summing up French bawdry*

The damage to Britain's reputation is enormous –
not because the Prince and Princess have chosen to
live apart, but because their separation is treated so
seriously.
Roy Hattersley, MP, *referring to the Prince and Princess
of Wales, the* Daily Mail, *December 1992*

RESPECT

The kingly office is entitled to no respect. It was
originally procured by highwayman's methods; it
remains a perpetuated crime, can never be anything
but the symbol of crime. It is no more entitled to
respect than is the flag of a pirate.
Mark Twain, Notebook

REVENGE

No more tears now; I will think upon revenge.
Mary Queen of Scots, *on hearing of the murder of her
secretary, David Riccio by her husband, Lord Darnley*

He would break a political opponent without pity,
but he was never needlessly cruel, and was glad to
treat foes no longer dangerous with contempt or
indifference. He wasted no time on minor revenges.
His sole vendetta was with Louis XIV.
Winston Churchill (1874-1965), *English statesman,
referring to William III*

REVOLUTION

Sir, listen to us. It is your business to listen to us.
You are a traitor. You have always deceived us and
are still doing so. But beware, the cup is brimming
over and the people are wearying of acting as your
bauble.
Louis Legendre, *Paris butcher, to Louis XVI*

I can see that M. De Lafayette wishes to save us, but
who will save us from M. De Lafayette?
Queen Marie Antoinette

If the insurgents murder me it will be a blessing, a
rescue from a most wretched existence.
Marie Antoinette, *to Mme Campen, refusing an offer of
body armour*

Madame is mounting in her tower
Who knows when she'll descend.
Paris street song, referring to Marie Antoinette

REWARD

I have deserved a thousand deaths.
John Dudley, *Duke of Northumberland (1502-53).
Known as the butcher, he was beheaded for his part in the
conspiracy to place Lady Jane Grey on the throne*

RHYME

And where is 'Fum' the Fourth, our 'royal bird'?
Gone down, it seems to Scotland to be fiddled
Unto by Sawney's violin, we have heard:
'Caw me, caw thee' – for six months hath been
hatching
This scene of royal itch and loyal scratching.
Lord Byron, *of George IV*, Don Juan canto IX

'Ave you 'eard o' the Widow at Windsor,
    For a hairy gold crown on 'er 'ead?
She 'as ships on the foam – she 'as millions at 'ome,
    An' she pays us poor beggars in red.

Walk wide o' the Widow at Windsor,
    for 'alf o' Creation she owns:
We 'ave bought 'er the same with the sword an' the
flame,
An' we've salted it down with our bones.
Rudyard Kipling *(1895-1936), English writer, of Queen
Victoria*, The Widow at Windsor

What is the rhyme for porringer?
What is the rhyme for porringer?
The king he had a daughter fair
And gave the Prince of Orange her.
Anon., *nursery rhyme, of King William III*

RICH

O, what a world of vile,
ill-favoured faults,
Looks handsome in three hundred
pounds a year.
Anne in The Merry Wives of Windsor *by* **William Shakespeare**

RISK

It is one of the incidents of the profession.
Umberto I *of Italy (1844-1900), after an attempt on his life*

RIVALRY

He only treats me to derive an advantage in his
future negotiations with his subjects.
Louis XIV, *referring to Charles II of England, in a letter to Barildon, 1680*

And when we open our dykes, the waters are ten
feet deep.
Wilhemina *(1880-1962), Queen of the Netherlands, replying to the boast of Wilhelm II of Germany that his guardsmen were all seven feet all*

The Admiral of the Atlantic salutes the Admiral of
the Pacific.
Wilhelm I, in a telegram sent to Tsar Nicholas II during a naval exercise, E. Crankshaw, The Shadow of the Winter Palace

ROMANCE

They met on the polo field. Where else does one meet people?'
Sarah Ferguson's mother, *on the first meeting of her daughter and Prince Andrew*

How can I be a maid and sleep every night with the King? When he comes to bed he kisses me, takes me by the hand and bids me 'Goodnight, sweetheart', and in the morning, he kisses me and bids me 'Farewell Darling'. Is not this enough?
Anne of Cleves (1515-57), *fourth wife of Henry VIII, on being asked by her lady-in-waiting if she was still a maid*

The constant presence of the little sister [Princess Margaret] who was far from understanding, and liked a good deal of attention herself, was not helping the romance.
Marion Crawford, *on the courtship of Prince Philip and Princess Elizabeth*

He is straight out of one of my mother's novels, don't you think.
Raine Spencer (stepmother of Diana), *referring to her future husband, May 1993*

I firmly believe Englishmen make the best husbands. With Frenchmen you wake up in the morning and wonder which girl they will go off with next.
Dame Barbara Cartland, *romantic novelist speaking of her daughter Raine's plans to marry a French Count*

ROYALTY

Royalty is a government in which the attention of the nation is concentrated on one person doing interesting actions.
Walter Bagehot (1826-77), *English economist and critic*

Royalty is a neurosis.
Get well soon.
Adrian Mitchell, *British poet, in a poem for the Prince of Wales*

The royal refuge our breed restores
With foreign courtiers and with foreign whores,
And carefully repeopled us again
Throughout his lazy, long, lascivious reign.
Daniel Defoe *(1661-1731), of Charles II*

Pete: Do you know, at this very moment, Her
Majesty is probably exercising the royal
prerogative.
Dud: What's that then, Pete?
Pete: Don't know the royal prerogative? It's a
wonderful animal, Dud. It's a legendary beast, half
bird, half fish, half unicorn, and it's being exercised
at this very moment.
   Do you know that legend has it that e'r so long as
the royal prerogative lives, happiness and laughter
will reign throughout this green and pleasant land.
Dud: And the yeoman will stand tall upon this
sceptred isle, Pete.
Peter Cooke and Dudley Moore, *The Dagenham
Dialogues, 1971*

We're the envy of the world, we are, having a Royal
Family. It's the one thing in the world no one else
has got. An' don't talk to me about Norway, and
Holland, and Sweden and all that rubbish.
   I'm talking about *Royalty.* Not bloody cloth-cap
kings riding about on bikes. I mean, that's not
Royalty. You'll never see our Queen on a bike. She
wouldn't demean herself.
Johnny Speight, The Thoughts of Chairman Alf (Alf
Garnett's Little Blue Book, *1973)*

Royalty does good and is badly spoken of.
Antisthenes *(c. 455-c. 360BC)*

Vulgarity in a king flatters the majority of the
nation.
George Bernard Shaw

Altogether the cost to the state of the monarchy is
probably not less than two million pounds a year –
as much as Omo and Daz spend on advertising.
Anthony Sampson, *British journalist and author, 1965*

The most interesting fact about the royal family today is its popularity, a popularity that is so deep-rooted, so complete and so unquestioned that it's hard to think that it might ever have been otherwise.
Andrew Morton, *introduction to* Fodor's Royalty Watching, *1987*

Ten years on, it is hard to remember how the royal family ever managed without Diana, Princess of Wales. With her youth, her openness, her photogenic charms, she has single-handedly rejuvenated not just her husband but an institution . . . thanks in large part to Diana, the British crown approaches the 21st century as popular as at any time in its history.
Anthony Holden, *author,* Charles and Diana, *1991*

The omens for the future of the monarchy are not good.
Anthony Holden, *biographer of the Prince of Wales, May, 1993*

She's not a real princess, she's a slap-them-on-the-bottom princess.
Earl Spencer, *of Sarah Ferguson*

Look, it's our *Dallas*, our serial, and they are our Kennedys, and we didn't invent any of it. The scenario is beyond belief.
Roger Therond, Paris Match, *1984*

There is not a single crowned head in Europe whose talents or merit would entitled him to be elected a vestryman by the people of any parish in America.
Thomas Jefferson *(1743-1826), president of the United States*

RULERS

The art of governing is a great métier, requiring the whole man, and therefore not well for a ruler to have too strong tendencies for other affairs.
Goethe *(1749-1832), German poet, dramatist, scientist and court official, Johann Peter Eckermann*, Conversations with Goethe

The rule is not so much a question of the heavy hand as the firm seat.
José Ortega Y Gasset (1883-1955), *Spanish writer and philosopher,* The Revolt of the Masses, *1930*

Not the least of the qualities that go into the marking of a great ruler is the ability of letting others serve him.
Cardinal Richelieu *(1585-1642), French prelate and statesman,* Political Testament, *1687*

If you have but a single ruler, you lie at the discretion of a master who has no reason to love you; and if you have several you must hear at once their tyranny and their divisions.
Jean Jacques Rousseau *(1712-78), French political philosopher, educationist and author, 1758*

Ill can he rule the great
that cannot reach the small.
Edmund Spenser *(c. 1552-99), English poet,* The Faerie Queen, *1596*

Every ruler is harsh whose rule is new.
Aeschylus, *(c. 525-c. 456 BC), Greek tragedian,* Prometheus Bound, *c.478BC*

Many have ruled well who could not perhaps define a commonwealth.
Sir Thomas Browne, *(1605-82), English author and physician,* Christian Morals, *1716*

Who rules the Kingdom? The King!
Who rules the King? The Duke!
Who rules the Duke! The Devil!
Anon., *contemporary graffiti (referring to Charles I and George Villiers, First Duke of Buckingham and a royal favourite*

Who would not be thy subject, James, t'obey
    A Prince, that rules by 'example, more than sway?
Whose manners draw, more then they powers constraine.
Ben Jonson, *of James I and VI,* Epigrammes

I can do no more than to implore virtuous ladies . . .
to rouse themselves and to show the world that even
if our sex were not born to command, we ought not
to be despised as companions (whether in public or
in private) of those who are born to rule; to rule and
to be obeyed.
Louise Labe (1524-66), *French poet, feminist, soldier,*
September 1548

RUMOUR

The whole affair has been built up from a molehill
into a mountain. I can definitely state that there is
no romance. They are just very good chums.
Inspector Paul Officer, in a statement to the press
denying the existence of a relationship between Prince
Charles and Lady Jane Wellesley who had holidayed
together in Granada (before the Prince's marriage)

He makes me laugh. He seems like the big brother
I've never had. He's fabulous, but I am not in love
with him. There is no question of me being the
future Queen of England. I don't think he's met her
yet.
Sarah Spencer, sister of the future Princess of Wales in an
interview, 1978

CHARLES TO MARRY ASTRID – OFFICIAL
Headline in the Daily Express *predicting a marriage between*
Prince Charles and Princess Marie-Astrid of Luxembourg,
1976

. . . They are not getting engaged this Monday, next
Monday, the Monday after, or any other Monday,
Tuesday, Wednesday or Thursday. They do not
know each other, and people who do not know each
other do not get engaged. The Royal Family do not
go in for arranged marriages. If the Prince and
Princess have met at all, then it has been briefly at
official functions.
John Dauth, press secretary to Prince Charles, denying the
existence of a romance between Prince Charles and Princess
Marie-Astrid of Luxembourg

The whole thing was planned like a military operation.
Prince Charles, *describing how the Queen Mother helped Charles and Diana meet at her home at Birkhall in secrecy before they officially announced their engagement*

If the rumour is true then I am deeply saddened by the news and I wish the Duke and Duchess of York the very best of luck.
Steve Wyatt, *who was romantically linked to the Duchess of York, in a statement after the announcement of her separation, March 1992*

SADNESS

Sound as also his head, which was very full of brains; but his blood was wonderfully tainted with melancholy.
Anon., *post-mortem on James I and VI*

'I will have no melancholy in this house' is her formula – and not a bad one either in moments of anxiety.
A.J. Balfour *(1848-1930), Scottish statesman and philosopher, referring to Queen Victoria in a letter to Lord Salisbury, 19 December 1899*

It was so awfully pathetic seeing her drawn on a gun carriage by the eight cream-coloured horses of Jubilee renown – but I never at any funeral felt so strongly before, that she herself was not on the bier but watching it all from somewhere and rejoicing in her people's loyalty
Kathleen Isherwood, *of Queen Victoria, 3 February 1901*

It's all very sad. They [Charles and Diana] clearly have been seeking friendships outside marriage, living separate lives, for a number of years. They either knew about each other's activities or didn't care, but either way the marriage has been a sham for a long time. Presumably they stayed together for the sake of the children, or the sake of the monarchy or both.
Penny Junor, *royal author,* Today, *January 1993*

SATISFACTION

I was not at all nervous, and had the satisfaction of learning that people were satisfied with what I had done and how I had done it.
Queen Victoria, *after holding her first Privy Council as Queen, June 1837*

SCOLD

That's right! You tell him!
The Queen, *to dinner guests, applauding them for being brave enough to argue with Prince Philip*

SCOTS

Lord Aberdeen was quite touched when I told him I was so attached to the dear, dear Highlands and missed the fine hills so much. There is a great peculiarity about the Highlands and Highlanders; and they are a such a chivalrous, fine, active people.
Queen Victoria

Where beats the heart so kindly as beneath the tartan plaid.
William Edmonstoune Aytoun *(1818-65), Scottish poet and humourist, of Prince Charles Edward Stuart at Versailles, 1849*

SCRUTINY

. . . Her manner and demeanour deserve all that is said of her, taste, a feeling of good breeding, and her looks, in my judgement, far exceed the most favourable account I heard.

Though not a beauty and not a good figure, she is really in person, in face, and especially in eyes and complexion, a very nice girl and quite such as might tempt.
Lord Holland,, *member of the Privy Council, describing Queen Victoria after a private meeting with her*

No institution should expect to be free from the scrutiny of those who give it their loyalty. But that scrutiny can be just as effective if it is made with a touch of gentleness, good humour and understanding. This sort of questioning can also act as an effective engine for change.
The Queen, at a Guildhall lunch, 24 November 1992

SELF KNOWLEDGE

I am more afraid of making a fault in my Latin than of the kings of Spain, France and Scotland, the whole house of Guise and all their confederates.
Elizabeth I

I'm as thick as a plank.
Princess Diana, 1970s

I know my own heart to be entirely English.
Queen Anne, drawing a contrast between herself and her predecessor, the Dutchman, William II, in a speech on the opening of Parliament, 1702

Although I may not be a lioness, I am a lion's cub, and inherit many of his qualities.
Elizabeth I

I do not keep a dog and bark myself.
Elizabeth I

I know I have the body of a weak and feeble woman, but I have the heart and stomach of a king, and of the King of England too.
Elizabeth I, in a speech at Tilbury, on the approach of the Spanish Armada

I will be good.
Queen Victoria, on seeing a chart of the line of succession to the throne for the first time, March 1830

He that would govern others, first should be the master of himself.
Philip Massinger (1583-1640), English dramatist, The Bondman, c.1624

I am the state.
Louis XIV, *attrib., in a remark before the French parliament, 1651*

According to him every person was to be bought: but some people haggled more about the price than others; and when his haggling was very obstinate and very skilful, it was called by some fine name. The chief trick by which clever men kept up the price of their abilities, was called integrity. The chief trick by which handsome women kept up the price of their beauty was called modesty. The love of God, the love of country, the love of family, the love of friends, were phrases of the same sort, delicate and convenient synonyms for the love of self. Thinking thus of mankind, Charles naturally cared very little what they thought of him. Honour and shame were scarcely more to him than light and darkness to the blind.
T.B. Macaulay, *of Charles II*, History of England

. . . Give yourself more . . . rest from the everlasting functions and speeches which get on one's nerves. I warned you what it would be like, these people think one is made of stone and that one can go on forever.
George V, *in a letter to the Prince of Wales, 12 October 1919*

Think – always think. After the last year, I've certainly learned I've got to think a lot more before I make a move, because I cannot go through another year like this year – just too much stress. And of course I brought it on myself. Therefore I must be responsible for that.
The Duchess of York, *when asked what action she would take to avoid adverse publicity in the future, 1992*

SEPARATION

While researching the book the volatility and turbulence in the marriage was very apparent to me. By the hour I was getting reports coming through to me that the Princess wanted to leave the royal family. We brought publication forward from September to June because the situation was so uncertain.
Andrew Morton, *referring to his book* Diana Her True Story, *and denying claims that his book was to blame for the separation of the royal couple, December 1992*

It's been general knowledge for ages. I think we're all bored by it. I certainly am.
Michael Parkinson, *radio/TV personality, speaking of the deteriorating relationship between Prince Charles and Princess Diana*

It's something that we'd all been led to expect.
Susan Hampshire, *actress, on the news of the separation of Charles and Diana*

I believe in the importance of concealment in these matters and, if you like, of hypocrisy.
Charles Moore, *editor of the* Sunday Telegraph, *referring to the publicity surrounding the marriage to the Prince and Princess of Wales, December 1992*

The fact is that, with great sadness, the Prince and Princess have recognised that their relationship would be better under separate domestic arrangements. They are still fond of one another. And they are fully supportive of one another's intentions to fulfil their individual duties as wholeheartedly as before.
A Palace spokesman, announcing the separation of the Prince and Princess of Wales

The most significant event in the background to yesterday's announcement was the publication of Morton's book. That was not a case of intrusion by the press, but of mind-boggling indiscretions by certain friends of the Princess of Wales. The media cannot reasonably be blamed for reporting such a story.
John Grigg, The Times, *December 1992*

I see no great harm in the book. Mr Morton did a professional job of work. It could not have been written without the ready testimony of many of the Princess of Wales's friends.
Bill Deedes, the Daily Telegraph, *December 1992*

ANNOUNCEMENT OF THE ROYAL SEPARATION AROUND THE WORLD, DECEMBER, 1992:

11 Years of Love, Romance and Tears. And now for him, hunting, fishing and water colour painting. For her, rock music, fashion and freedom.
Announcement in a French newspaper

It not only benefits Charles and Diana, but the prestige of the crown.
El Mundo *(Spain)*

Di's sacrifice for England: A marriage with no husband.
Headline in BZ *newspaper (Germany)*

Splitting Heirs
Headline in the New York Post

SERVANTS

There are only two kinds of people in the world: those who are nice to their servants and those who aren't.
Duke of Arygll, attrib.

SEX

I'm not a social person but I could fall for a Duke –
they are a great aphrodisiac.
Tina Brown, Tatler, 1979

Mr Pierce did also tell me as a great truth, as being
told it by Mr Cowly who was by and heard it – that
Tom Killigrew should publicly tell the King that his
matters were coming into a very ill state, but that yet
there was a way to help all – which is, says he,
'There is a good honest able man that I could name,
that if your Majesty would imploy and command to
see all things well executed, all things would soon be
mended; and this is one Charles Stuart – who now
spends his time in imploying his lips and his prick
about the Court, and hath no other imployment.
But if you could give him this imployment, he were
the fittest man in the world to perform it. 'This he
says is most true.'
Samuel Pepys, of Charles II, Diary, 8 December 1666

The Empress Massalina tir'd in lust at least,
But you could never satisfy this beast.
Cleveland I say, was much to be admir'd
For she was never satisfied or tired.
Full forty men a day have swived the shore,
Yet like a bitch she wags her tail for more.
John Lacy, of Barbara Villiers, Countess of Castlemaine,
Duchess of Cleveland and mistress to Charles II, Satire

SEX APPEAL

We need heroes. Whether or not it pleases you, Mr
Connery, we have decided that you will be our hero.
Princess Anne, to Sean Connery

I've spent time with her and she's everything a man
could want. She's a very warm, beautiful, intelligent
and sexy lady.
Sylvester Stallone, of the Duchess of York

SINS

A branch of the sin of drunkenness, which is the root of all sins.
James I and VI, A Counterblast to Tobacco, *1604*

God in his wrath sent Saul to trouble Jewry,
And George to England in a greater fury;
For George in sin as far exceedeth Saul
As every Bishop Burnet did Saint Paul.
Anon., *of George I*

I hope never again to commit a mortal sin, not even a venial one, if I can help it.
Charles VIII, *King of France (1470-98) son and successor of Louis XI*

SMOKING

Herein is not only a great vanity, but a great contempt of God's good gifts, that the sweetness of man's breath, being a good gift of god, should be wilfully corrupted by this stinky smoke.
James I and VI, *on smoking*

My Lord Montjoy, reprehended by the King for taking tobacco, answered, 'By that your Majesty shall have a little practice in England, you will find greater faults to pardon amongst us.'
Sir Henry Wotton *(1568-1639), of James I and VI*, Table Talk

A custom loathsome to the eye, hateful to the nose, harmful to the brain, dangerous to the lungs, and in the black, stinky fume thereof, nearest resembling the horrible stygian smoke of the pit that is bottomless.
King James I and VI, *of smoking*

SONG

A careless song with a little nonsense now and then, does not misbecome the monarch.
Horace Walpole

SOVEREIGNTY

To appear at church every Sunday; to look down upon, and let himself be looked at for an hour by the congregation, is the best means of becoming popular which can be recommended to a young sovereign.
Goethe, *Johann Peter Eckermann*, Conversations with Goethe, *April 2 1829*

Whom hatred frights
Let him not dream of sovereignty.
Ben Jonson, Sejanus, His Fall, *1603*

If a sovereign oppresses his people to a great degree, they will rise and cut off his head.
There is a remedy in human nature against tyranny that will keep us safe under every form of government.
Samuel Johnson, *James Boswell*, Life of Samuel Johnson, *March 31 1772*

SPORT

If I hit a bad shot no tutting please.
Prince Andrew, *to crowd at the first tee at the Monarch's Course, Gleneagles, May 1993*

My partner played a lot better than I did. If he has time to work at the game he can become a very good player.
Jack Nicklaus, *after playing with Prince Andrew at the opening of the Monarch's course at Gleneagles. The Prince played a decisive eight-foot putt on the 18th green*

The King bathes, and with great success; a machine follows the royal one into the sea, filled with fiddlers, who play *God Save the King* as his majesty takes his plunge.
Fanny Burney *(Frances Burney D'Arblay) (1752-1840), British novelist, referring to George III at Weymouth, Diary, 8 July 1789*

STARS

Ah, the one with the Robert Redford looks?
Prince Charles's *standard response when asked about his younger brother, Andrew*

We're three big blondes.
Princess Michael of Kent, *referring to herself, Maria Aitken, the actress, and Anna Raphael, the TV director. All three are making a documentary based on Princess Michael's book,* The Empress and the Architect, *September 1992*

Kings are like stars – they rise and set, they have the worship of the world but no repose.
Percy Bysshe Shelley, Hellas, *1821*

STRATEGY

If Louis XVI had shown himself on horseback he would have won.
Napoleon Bonaparte, *referring to the massacre at the Tuileries, 1792*

STRENGTH

What stronger breastplate than a heart untainted!
Thrice is he armed that hath his quarrel just,
And he but naked, though locked up in stell,
Whose conscience with injustice is corrupted.
King Henry in Henry IV Part II, *by* **William Shakespeare**
Shakespeare

If a lion knew his own strength, hard were it for any
man to rule him.
Sir Thomas More, *attrib, of Henry VIII*

Go, gentlemen, every man unto his charge:
Let not our babbling dreams affright our souls;
Conscience is but a word cowards use,
Devis'd at first to keep the strong in awe;
Our strong arms be our conscience, swords our law.
March on, join bravely, let us to't pell-mell;
If not to heaven, then hand in hand to hell.
Richard II

SUPPORT

My nature is too passionate; my emotions too
fervent, and I am a person who has to cling to
someone in order to find peace and contentment.
Queen Victoria, *of her need for her husband's support*

SURPRISE

He widdled all over me.
Prince Philip, *to surprised fellows of the Zoological Society
after approaching an orang-utan at London Zoo, 1967*

I *was* a bit surprised to see the Princess flying in club
class while I was up in first class – but I guess that's
the way it goes.
Paul Raymond, *porn-king, on Princess Diana*

SYCOPHANCY

Let us be clear about this: if legislation is framed
which means that the royal family can only be
reported upon in terms of drivelling and lying
sycophancy, the royal family is doomed.
Republicanism will at least become respectable.
The Evening Standard, *commenting on press censorship,*
January 1993

TALENT

My only excuse for being so various is that I appear
as 'chemist, fiddler, statesman and buffoon' entirely
by request.
Prince Philip

No one dances better, no man runs or jumps better.
Indeed he jumped higher than ever Englishmen did
in so short a time, from a private gentleman to a
dukedom.
Arthur Wilson, *of George Villiers,* First Duke of
Buckingham, The History of Great Britain

He had no favourites and indeed no friends, having
none of that expansion of heart, none of those
amiable connecting talents, which are necessary for
both. This, together with the sterility of his
conversation, made him prefer the company of
women, with whom he rather sauntered away than
enjoyed his leisure hours. He was addicted to
women, but chiefly to such as require little attention
and less pay.
Lord Chesterfield, *of George II*

Your Majesty's life has been passed in constant
communion with great men, and the knowledge and
management of important transactions. Even if your
Majesty were not gifted with those great abilities,
which all must now acknowledge, this rare and
choice experiment must give your Majesty an
advantage in judgement, which few living persons,
and probably no living Prince can rival.
Benjamin Disraeli, *letter to Queen Victoria, 26 February*
1868

TALES OF THE TAPE

In the 1,574-word tape, the couple speak for six minutes, often in graphic detail. They spend around a minute saying goodbye to each other, blowing kisses and calling each other 'darling' before hanging up. During the loving chat, these are some of the intimate phrases used by them.

Darling	She: 17 times	He: 7 times
I love you	She: 12 times	He: twice
Adore you	She: –	He: once
etc.		

Details of the alleged Camillagate tape, published in Today, *January 1993*

TALL STORIES

No women came amiss to him if they were willing and very fat. The standard of his majesty's taste made all those ladies who aspired to his favour and who were near the stateable size strain and swell themselves like frogs in the fable to rival the bulk of the ox. Some succeeded and others burst.
Lord Chesterfield, *of George I*

It has been said, not truly, but with a possible approximation to truth, that in 1802 every hereditary monarch was insane.
Walter Bagehot

Obviously someone didn't like someone else very much and gave them a straight left. He went whizzing through the window and the police and ambulance had to be called. Otherwise the lunch was a great success.
Lord Snowdon, *ex-husband of Princess Margaret, in New York for the American launch of his new book, speaking of an incident in a New York restaurant where he was having lunch*

I've got a grenade and a gun in my bag.
Lord Linley, *quoted in the* Mail on Sunday *under the headline* ROYAL 'JOKE' TRIGGERS AIRPORT SECURITY ALERT, *May 1993*

TAXATION

All money nowdays seems to be produced with a natural homing instinct for the Treasury.
Prince Philip

Reactions from MPs who were incensed that the government had ignored surveys showing the majority of Britons want the royal family to pay tax (1992):

People will be furious about this. It is wrong that the richest woman in the world should not pay tax.
Eric Clark

There is no doubt that most people would like to see the Queen pay tax. Many members of the royal family are living off the taxpayers' money. The grave economic situation should be recognised by the royal family. It is up to them now to express a willingness to make a contribution through the tax system.
Denis Canavan, *Falkirk West*

This aggravates the situation of the monarchy and could, in the long run, put it in jeopardy.
Andrew Mackinley, *Thurrock*

Why should the Queen – a billionaire – not pay tax when her subjects on miniscule incomes do.
Robert Hughes, *Aberdeen North*

The increase of the 'black' economy shows that people do not, once they are freed of their companies, their unions and to a certain extent their government, shirk the idea of work.
Prince Charles, *'Sayings of the Week'*, *the* Observer, *22 November 1981*

Except taxes!
Elizabeth Bonaparte (1785-1879), *sister-in-law of Napoleon, on her deathbed, in reply to someone who said that nothing was as sure as death*

TEMPER

The key is never to let him down, and if you make a mistake be honest. I always make a point of saying that to the new equerries. Remember, be honest. Because he'll always see through it. And if you get ticked off by Prince Philip, you know you've been ticked off.
Geoff Williams, *personal pilot to Prince Phillip*

He was recording some television interview, and there was a glass of water beside his chair. It wasn't cold enough, so when the interview continued the next day I asked if they could be sure to provide cold water.

He suddenly turned on me in front of everyone, and snapped, 'I'll do my own complaining, thank you.'

I was so upset I nearly resigned. He really hurt me.
One of Prince Philip's private secretaries

TEMPTATION

I was attractive. That was the halfway house to temptation, and in such cases human nature does the rest. To tempt and to be tempted is much the same thing.
Catherine the Great, *writing of the legitimacy of her son and heir*

His prayer 'lead us not into temptation' must have been uttered with a feeling akin to hopelessness.
Report of Edward VII's accession to the throne in The Times

THREATS

I will make you shorter by the head.
Elizabeth I

I cannot be indifferent to the assassination of a
member of my profession. We should be obliged to
shut up business if we, the kings, were to consider
the assassination of kings as of no consequence at
all.
Edward VII, *refusing to recognise the Karageorgevic
regime in Serbia after the murder of King Alexander and the
extermination of the Obrenovic dynasty, 1903*

THRONE

A doubtful throne is ice on summer seas.
Alfred, Lord Tennyson, The Coming of Arthur, Idylls of
the King, *1869*

What is the throne? – a bit of wood gilded and
covered in velvet. I am the state – I alone am here
the representative of the people. Even if I had done
wrong you should not have reproached me in public
– people wash their dirty linen at home. France has
more need of me than I of France.
Napoleon I, *to the Senate, 1814*

TIME

Go Sir, gallop, and don't forget that the world was
made in six days. You can ask me for anything you
like, except time.
Napoleon I, *to an aide, 1803, R.M. Johnson*, The Corsican

Soldiers, from the summit of yonder pyramids forty
centuries look down upon you.
Napoleon I, *in Egypt, 21 July 1798*

Whatever shall we do in that remote spot? Well, we
will write our memoirs. Work is the scythe of time.
Napoleon I, *on board HMS* Bellerophon, *August 1815*

Prince Philip is not a morning man. He's not really civilised until after nine. None the less, he rises early and breakfasts well.
Royal equerry, *of Prince Philip*

TRAGEDY

At the opening of the year 1536 Anne Boleyn's position rested on two supports: the life of Catherine of Aragon and the prospect of a Prince. Never was fortune more cruel. On January 7th Catherine died, and on the 29th, the day of the funeral, Anne gave premature birth to a male child. She had miscarried of her saviour.

The tragedy must obviously move to a close; and it moved swiftly. On May 2nd she was arrested and sent to the tower, accused of adultery with five men, one of whom was her brother. In the subsequent trials all were found guilty, and the law took its course.

Anne herself was executed on May 18th. Whether she was guilty or not, no human judgement can now determine, and contemporaries differed. In all probability she had been indiscreet. If she had gone further, if she had really committed adultery – and that possibly cannot be lightly dismissed – then it is likely that a desperate woman had taken a desperate course to save herself from ruin.

Whatever the truth, she had played her game and lost.
J.E. Neale, Queen Elizabeth

Fate wrote her a most tremendous tragedy, and she played it in tights.
Max Beerbohm *(1872-1956), English writer and caricaturist, of Caroline, Queen consort to George IV*, King George the Fourth

TRAINING

You can do a lot if you have been properly trained,
and I hope I have been.
The Queen

Training isn't necessary. They do on-the-job
training, so to speak, and learn the trade, or
business or craft, just from being with us and
watching us function, and seeing the whole
organisation around us. They can't avoid it. What
is much more difficult is bringing them up as people.
Prince Philip, *on preparing children for royal duties*

TRAVEL

There is no need to forbid young men to travel for
fear they may abscond, if we make their native
country attractive to them.
Catherine the Great

I am weary of travelling and am resolved to go
abroad no more. But when I am dead and gone, I
know not what my brother will do: I am much
afraid that when he comes to wear the Crown he
will be obliged to travel again. And yet I will take
care to leave my Kingdoms to him in peace, wishing
he may keep them long so. But this hath all of my
fears, little of my hopes, and less of my reason.
Charles II, *of James II, Christopher Falkus,* Charles II

I return a thorough optimist. When one has
travelled over the vast extent of the Empire . . . it is
impossible to despair of the future of the British
race.
The Duke of York, *returning after a world tour, 1927*

TRIBUTES

On the death of King George VI:

. . . He was essentially broad-minded and was ready
to accept changes that seemed necessary.
Clement Attlee *(1883-1967), Prime Minister*

Modest and gentle, he gave a moral lead to all his
people.
The Evening Standard

Not at all palace minded, but with the right dignity
of kings and an upholder of the decencies. This was
by any standards, anywhere, a good man.
The Daily Mirror

We have lost a great bloke.
Australian MP, attrib.

King George represented the civic virtues of the
British people, and exercised them with simplcity
and a high sense of duty.
Alcide de Gasperi *(1891-1954), Italian Prime Minister*

Never have we felt the loss of a foreign monarch so
deeply.
Van Houte, *Belgian Prime Minister*

King George carries out noble traditions with
dignity and greatness, and devotion.
Edgar Faure *(1908-88), French Prime Minister*

He was a very great man, and his loss will be felt the
world over. He was a staunch friend of this country,
and Winston will feel his loss most of all in his
dealings with Stalin.
King George VI, *referring to the death of President
Roosevelt*, Diary, *1945*

TROUBLE

Will no one rid me of this turbulent priest?
Henry II (1133-89), *referring to Thomas Becket,*
Archbishop of Canterbury. Four of Henry's household
knights took these words literally, hurried to Canterbury and
killed Becket in the cathedral, December 1170

TRUE CONFESSIONS

I'm self-employed.
Prince Philip

I still love you, but in politics there is no heart, only
head.
Napoleon I, *referring to his divorce, for reasons of state,*
from Empress Josephine, 1800. C. Barnett, Bonaparte

TRUST

I just trust too many people. I'm too spontaneous
and I don't think before I act.
The Duchess of York, *in an interview with* Hello
magazine, August 1990

A prince who will not undergo the difficulty of
understanding must undergo the danger of trust.
George Savile, *Marquis of Halifax*

Put not your trust in princes.
Bible, *Psalms*

Here lies our Sovereign Lord, the King
Whose word no man relies on:
He never says a foolish thing
Nor ever does a wise one.
John Wilmot, *Earl of Rochester, written on the door of*
Charles II's bedchamber

TRUTH

It is impossible that a man who is false to his friends and neighbours should be true to the public.
Bishop Berkeley, Maxims, Concerning Patriotism, *1750*

The plain truth is, that he was a most intolerable ruffian, a disgrace to human nature, and a blot of blood and grease upon the History of England.
Charles Dickens, *of Henry VIII*, A Child's History of England

There is no truth whatever in the story that Prince Charles had sold his autograph at any time. There is also no truth whatever in the story that he sold his composition book to a classmate. In the first place he is intelligent and old enough to realise how embarrassing this would turn out to be, and second, he is only too conscious of the interest of the press in anything to do with himself and his family. The suggestion that his parents keep him so short of money that he has to find other means to raise it is also a complete invention. Finally, the police would not have attempted to regain the composition book unless they were quite satisfied that it had been obtained illegally.
A denial sent by the Queen's press secretary to Time *magazine who had printed the story about Prince Charles selling his composition book to a fellow pupil at Gordonstoun in 1964*

MONEYED PRINCE CHARLIE
The royal family's press officer mounts a princely defence in his belated offer to clarify the case.
The headline used by Time *magazine for the denial letter, above*

TYRANTS

We wish we had rather endured thee (O Charles)
than have been condemned to this mean tyrant
[(Cromwell] not that we desire any kind of slavery,
but that the quality of the master something
graces the condition of the slave.
Edward Sexby, *of Charles I,* Killing No Murder

In the first year of freedom's second dawn
Died George the Third; although no tyrant one
Who shielded tyrants, till each sense withdrawn
Left him nor mental nor external sun:
A better farmer ne'er brushed dew from lawn,
A worse king never left a realm undone!
He died but left his subjects still behind,
One half as mad and t'other no less blind.
Lord Byron, *on the death of George III,* The Vision of
Judgement

VICES

Society punishes not the vices of its members, but
their detection.
Countess of Blessington *(1789-1849), Irish writer*

A prince should be prudent enough to avoid the
scandal of vices that could lose him the state.
Niccolò Machiavelli

I have never feared temptation with regard to
women because I have no inclination in that respect,
and that species of vice disgusts me.
Prince Albert

VICTORY

I will not be exhibited in his triumph.
Cleopatra, *remark concerning Octavian's victory, Arthur
Weigall,* The Life and Times of Cleopatra

Those which are victorious, Madame.
Napoleon I, *in reply to Madame Montholon who had
enquired what troops he considered the best, Bourrienne,*
Memoirs, *1829*

VIRGINITY

It will be quite sufficient for the memorial of my
name and for my glory if, when I die, an inscription
be engraved on a marble tomb, saying, 'Here lieth
Elizabeth, which reigned a virgin, and died a virgin.'
Elizabeth I, *in answer to a request by the speaker and the
lower house that she should marry*

They should have known he needed someone more
experienced. To hell with being a virgin. That was
the least important consideration.
*Royal insider, after the announcement of the separation of
Prince Charles and Princess Diana*

VIRTUE

Virtue, like a dowerless beauty, has more admirers
than followers.
Countess of Blessington

We owe subjection and obedience to our kings,
whether good or bad, alike, for that has respect unto
their office, but as to esteem and affection, these are
only due to their virtue.
Michael Eyquem de Montaigne, *'That Our Affections
Carry Themselves Beyond Us'*, Essays, *1580-88*

The finest and most poetic thing that can be said
about the Queen is . . . that her virtues and powers
are not those of a great woman, like Elizabeth or
Catherine II . . . but are the virtues and powers of an
ordinary woman; things that any person, however
humble, can appreciate and imitate . . . an example
inestimably precious to the whole world.
Alfred Munby, *of Queen Victoria*, Letter to Austin
Dobson, *4 July 1897*

WAR

We are not interested in the possibilities of defeat –
they do not exist.
Queen Victoria, *to A.J. Balfour, referring to the Boer War,*
December 1899

Russia still writhed and stumbled. The wave of
revolts and uprisings, and constant agitations, the
incessant inflammatory orations of men possessed
of little political competence had by this time cowed
the emperor and the ruling class into bewildered and
sullen inertia.
Maria, *Grand Duchess of Russia (1890-1958), referring to*
the Russian Revolution of 1917

Don't forget your great guns, which are the most
respectable arguments of the rights of Kings.
Frederick the Great, *King of Prussia*

I make war on the living, not on the dead.
Charles V, *Holy Roman Emperor, after the death of*
Martin Luther, when it was suggested that he hang the
corpse on the gallows

Rascals, would you live forever?
Frederick the Great, *King of Prussia, to reluctant soldiers*
at the battle of Kolin, June 1757

Great glory, equal to that of our old victories, was
won on that day. Some indeed say that there fell
little less than eighty thousand of the Britons, with a
loss of our soldiers of about four hundred, and only
as many wounded. Boadicea put an end to her life
by poison.
Tacitus *(c.44-c120AD), Roman historian,* Annals of
Boadicea

War is the trade of kings.
John Dryden *(1631-1700), English poet*

From the sublime to the ridiculous is but a step.
Napoleon I, *to the Abbé du Pradt, after the retreat from*
Moscow, 1812

The King loved working to rule. The War brought plenty of rules to which he could work. Certainly he took his duties as head of his household as seriously as any suburban father. During the blackout, he often stepped out into the courtyard to check whether any light was escaping from the Palace windows, and when it became necessary to conserve fuel, he insisted that the rooms of Windsor Castle and Buckingham Palace were kept in an appropriately chilly state. He even went round the family's bathrooms and marked the hot water limit, five inches from the bottom, in each bath (he painted the mark himself, having measured the distance with a foot ruler). Although he always appeared in public in uniform, he made do with his pre-war stock of clothes, of which he admittedly had a plentiful supply. When his clothes and cuffs wore out, he had new ones made from his shirt tails.
A.J.P. Taylor *(1906-90), English historian, of George VI*

It is most encouraging to know that it was possible for me to land on the Normandy beaches only ten days after D-Day.
George VI, *16 June 1944*

I am very worried over the general situation, as everything we try to do appears to be wrong and gets us nowhere.
George VI, *March 1940*

Après nous le deluge (after us the flood)
Madame de Pompadour, *after the Battle of Rossbach, 1757*

W E A K N E S S E S

The Tsar is not treacherous but he is weak. Weakness is not treachery, but it fulfils all its functions.
Wilhelm II, *King of Prussia and Emperor of Germany, referring to Nicholas II, March 1907*

I generally had to give in.
Napoleon I, *speaking of his relationship with Empress Josephine, May 1816*

WEALTH

Your Lord the King of England, who lacks nothing, has men, horses, gold, silk, jewels, fruits, game and everything else. We in France have nothing but bread, wine and gaiety.
Louis VII, *King of France (1120-80), to Walter Map. By 'France' Louis meant the area around Paris that he ruled directly. J. Gillingham*, Richard the Lionheart.

WEATHER

What a beautiful day.
Last words of **Alexander I**, *Tsar of Russia (1777-1825). The death of his natural daughter in 1824 helped break the heart of the Emperor who died in December 1825 in the seaport town of Taganaog*

Yes, it is indeed frightful weather for a journey as long as the one before me.
Last words of **Maria Theresa** *(1638-83), Queen Consort to Louis XIV of France, in reply to her son's comments on the rain*

WEDDING

I'm so proud of you and when you come up the aisle I'll be there at the altar for you tomorrow. Just look 'em in the eye and knock 'em dead.
Prince Charles, *in a note to Diana on the eve of their wedding.*

I feel very insulted. It has taken all the pleasure out of the day for me.
A Balmoral estate worker, referring to a letter from the estate administrator asking all workforce to 'dress properly' for the wedding of Princess Anne

The Duke of Edinburgh drove his Range Rover like
a mad thing from Aberdeen Airport to Balmoral.
Royal watchers, observing Prince Philip arriving for his
daughter's wedding, 1992

All right then?
Princess Anne, *to Prince Philip as they walked down the*
aisle at Balmoral, 12 December 1992

WIFE

When a man opens the car door for his wife, it's
either a new car or a new wife.
Prince Philip, *1988*

You have sent me a Flanders mare.
Henry VIII, *on meeting his fourth wife, Anne of Cleves, for*
the first time, generally assumed to have been said to Thomas
Cromwell

Damn the North, and damn the South, and damn
Wellington! The question is, how am I going to get
rid of this damned Princess of Wales?
George IV, *when Prince of Wales, W.M. Wilkins,* Mrs
Fitzherbert and George IV, *October 1811*

'Sir your bitterest enemy is dead.' 'Is she by god,'
said the tender husband.
George IV's *response to Sir Nagle's attempt to tell him of*
Napoleon's death, The Journal of Hon. Henry Edward Fox,
25 August 1821

Well, gentlemen since you will have it so – 'God
save the Queen', and may all your wives be like her!
G. Russell, *of Queen Caroline,* Collections and
Recollections

George I kept his wife in prison because he believed
that she was no better than he was.
Will Cuppy, The Decline and Fall of Practically Everybody

The Duke of York in all things but his amours was
led by the nose by his wife.
Samuel Pepys, *of Anne Hyde, Duchess of York,* Diary,
30 October 1668

Bluff Henry the Eighth to six spouses was wedded:
One died, one survived, two divorced, two
beheaded.
Anon., *Nursery rhyme, c.1750*

WILL

This is our gracious will.
Charles VIII, *King of France (1470-98) Royal Order of
12 March 1497*

WILLPOWER

Nature has a funny way of sending us what we most
resist. None of us can remain smugly immune from
addiction, whether it is chocolate, cigarettes,
alcohol, drugs or even work. Many will use these
addictive 'tools' to distract them from having to face
life in a changing and testing world.
Princess Diana, *at a charity lunch, 1992*

WISDOM

The wisest fool in Christendom.
Henri IV, *King of France, referring to James I and VI*

And what, in a mean man, I should call folly, is in
your majesty remarkable wisdom.
Philip Massinger, *of James I and VI*

He was a wise fellow that, being bid to ask what he
would of the king, desired to know none of his
secrets.
Pericles *by* **William Shakespeare**

A wise and prudent king knows how to make use of
even the least of his subjects.
Jean de La Fountaine

Wise men do not pick quarrels with the great.
Pierre de Beaumarchais, Le Marriage de Figaro

His mind was an open book where all who chose
might read, and he committed to paper more
indiscretions than any ruler in history.
Wilbur Cortez, *of Charles I, W.C. Abbot, Writings and
Speeches of Oliver Cromwell*

WIT

There is no marvel in a woman learning to speak,
but there would be in teaching her to hold her
tongue.
Elizabeth I

*Honi soit qui mal y pense. [Evil be to him who evil
thinks]*
Edward III, *attrib., on retrieving the Countess of
Salisbury's garter, which had fallen off. In later tradition,
associated with the foundation of the Order of the Garter,
1344*

We are not amused.
Queen Victoria, *upon seeing an imitation of herself by the
Honourable Alexander Grantham Yorke, groom-in-waiting
to the Queen*

A crown is merely a hat that lets the rain in.
Frederick the Great, *King of Prussia*

You write to me that is impossible, the word is not
French.
Napoleon I, *in a letter to General Lemarois, 9 July 1813*

See in what Glory Charles now sits
    With Truth to conquer Treason
And prove he is the King of Wits
    The world, himself and reason . . .

The King the four great Bills must pass
    And none but Saints are free
The Irish and Cavaliers, alas!
    Must th'only rebels be . . .

Thus Royal Charles lets to lease
    Lays sword and sceptre down
To shew he values us and Peace
    Above a glorious Crown.
Marchamont Nedham, *of Charles II*, A Short History of
the English Rebellion Compiled in Verse

His wit was not acquired by reading; that much he
had above his original stock by nature, was from
company, in which he was very capable to observe.
He could not so properly be said to have a wit very
much raised, as a plain, gaining, well-bred,
recommending kind of wit.
Marchamont Nedham, *of Charles II*

James's humour was a tumbling wit that turned
things upside down and heaped together
incongruous thoughts and images in a hurly-burly
jumble, as when he prayed the Pope to permit him
the hawking of the stream in purgatory. His mind
passed easily from topic to topic, and he applied the
vocabulary of one set of ideas to things entirely
different, throwing discordant images into
grotesque juxtaposition. His wit was the rollicking
foolery of the court jester, enriched by his extensive
knowledge.
D. Harris Wilson, *of James I and VI*, King James VI and I

They gave William IV a lovely funeral. It took six
men to carry the beer.
Louis Untermeyer, *A Treasury of Laughter*

194

WOMEN

But now it is not as a woman descending from noble ancestry, but as one of the people that I am avenging lost freedom, my scourged body, the outraged chastity of my daughters. Roman lust has gone so far that not our very persons, not even age or virginity, are left unpopulated . . . this is a woman's resolve; as for men, they may live and be slaves.
Boadicea, *(first century* AD), *Queen of Iceni (Norfolk, Suffolk and part of Cambridgeshire)*

I saw pale kings, and princes too,
pale warriors, death-pale were they all;
Who cry'd – La Belle Dame sans merci
Hath thee in thrall!
John Keats *(1795-1821), English poet,* La Belle Dame sans Merci

If things were even worse than they are after all this war they might have laid the blame upon the rule of a woman; but if such persons are honest they should blame only the rule of men who desire to play the part of kings. In future, if I am not any more hampered, I hope to show that women have a more sincere determination to preserve the country than those who have plunged it into the miserable condition to which it has been bought.
Catherine de Medici, *Italian-born Queen of France 1519-89, in a letter to the Ambassador of Spain, 1570*

It cam' wi' a lass, it will gang wi' a lass. [It came with a woman and it will go with one]
King James V *of Scotland (1512-42), attrib., although it is unlikely that James V spoke with a strong Scottish accent*

The Kingdom of the Romans endured much evil through Cleopatra, Queen of Egypt, that worst of women. And so with others. Therefore it is no wonder that the world now suffers through the malice of women.
Henrich Kramer and Jakob Sprenger, *German Dominican monks, of Cleopatra,* The Classic Study of Witchcraft, *1486*

195

The book is going well. I am enjoying following in the footsteps of a woman who showed such inspiration in her hunger for different places and cultures.

We also share the same sense of humour.
The Duchess of York, *referring to her book on Queen Victoria, 1992*

WORDS

Must! Is must a word to be addressed to Princes? Little man, little man! Thy father, if he had been alive, durst not have used that word.
Elizabeth I, to Robert Cecil

WORK

I used to lead a leisurely life, the life of a duchess, until I married and became a duchess. It's all work, work, work.
Duchess of Bedford

I think the most important thing for me at the moment is to keep a low profile, work hard and make sure that the charities are well supported.
The Duchess of York, *in a television interview referring to the recent publicity over her marital problems*

I don't think people realise just what I do put into a day.
The Duchess of York, *in an interview with David Frost, November 1987*

Being a King is a dangerous profession. But it is devilish well paid.
Alfonso of Spain, *cousin of Prince Albert Edward*

The work is entirely new to me and I find it rather difficult to begin with, but I shall get used to it.
Prince Albert, *as Officer Commanding No.4 Squadron, Boy Wing, Cranwell, 1918*

Gawking cockney at Buckingham Palace: He's a decent bloke, you know. Works hard. I wouldn't have his job.
GI Joe: Yeah, not much chance of promotion.
Time *magazine, 6 March 1944*

The pay is about the same as local hotels pay their chambermaids. But the work is rotten and no one wants to work for the royals these days . . . You have to let out his dirty bathwater and even make sure his toothpaste tube is squeezed from the bottom.
Royal worker, on why not one applicant had applied for the job of housekeeper to Prince Charles at Birkhall House. The job had been advertised for five months. Today, *June 1993*

I think she [the Duchess of York] is looking for a better accountant. I think she's hoping to find one at the United Nations.
Geoffrey Goodwin, *journalist, referring to the appointment of the Duchess of York as a goodwill ambassador to the United Nations*

They'll probably insist she wears boots to avoid further toe-sucking exercises.
Mike Carlton, *presenter on LBC morning show, after the announcement of the Duchess of York's UN appointment*

YOUTH

Youth, I forgive thee.
To his attendants:
Take off his chains, give him 100 shillings and let him go.
Richard I *(Richard the Lionheart), to Bertrand de Gourdon who shot him with an arrow*

Z

Thou whoreson Zed! Thou unnecessary letter!
King Lear in King Lear *by* **William Shakespeare**

INDEX